Taxcafe.co.uk Tax Guides

How to Avoid Property Tax

By Carl Bayley BSc ACA

Important Legal Notices:

TAXCafe™
TAX GUIDE – "How to Avoid Property Tax"

Published by:
Taxcafe UK Limited
4 Polwarth Gardens
Edinburgh EH11 1LW
Tel: (01592) 560081

Email address: team@taxcafe.co.uk

First Edition	March 2002
Second Edition	June 2002
Third Edition	September 2002
Fourth Edition	January 2003
Fifth Edition	April 2003
Sixth Edition	March 2004

ISBN 1 904608 13 2

About the Author

Carl Bayley is the author of a number of tax guides designed specifically for the layman. Carl's particular speciality is his ability to take the weird, complex and inexplicable world of taxation and set it out in the kind of clear, straightforward language that taxpayers themselves can understand. As he often says, 'my job is to translate tax into English'.

Carl takes the same approach when speaking on taxation, a role he has undertaken with some relish on a number of occasions, including his highly acclaimed series of seminars at the Evening Standard Homebuyer Show.

In addition to being a recognised author and speaker on the subject, he has also spoken on property taxation on BBC radio and television.

A chartered accountant by training, Carl began his professional life in 1983, in the Birmingham office of one of the 'Big 4' accountancy firms. He qualified as a double prize-winner and immediately began specialising in taxation.

After 17 years honing his skills with major firms, Carl began the new millennium in January 2000 by launching his own Edinburgh-based tax consultancy practice, Bayley Consulting, through which he now provides advice on a wide variety of UK taxation issues, especially property taxation, Inheritance Tax planning and matters affecting small and medium-sized businesses.

As well as being Taxcafe.co.uk's Senior Consultant, Carl is also Chairman of the Institute Members in Scotland group and a member of the governing Council of the Institute of Chartered Accountants in England and Wales.

When he isn't working, Carl takes on the equally taxing challenges of hill walking and writing poetry.

Dedication

As usual, this book is dedicated to the two very special ladies who have shaped my life:

To Isabel, whose unflinching support has seen me through the best and the worst.

And to Diana, who made it all possible.

Thanks

Sincere thanks are also due to my good friend and colleague, Nick, who believed in me long before I did.

C.B., Edinburgh, March 2004

Contents

Chapter 3 – How to Avoid Income Tax (Contd)

Chapter 4 – How to Avoid Capital Gains Tax   45

Introduction

By the author

This guide was first produced in March 2002, as a response to the huge demand for advice on property taxation issues which we had been experiencing at Taxcafe.co.uk. That demand has continued to grow at a phenomenal pace and is responsible for the fact that this guide is already in its sixth edition, just two years later, and has expanded rapidly to the six chapters which you have here.

People in the UK have invested in property for centuries. However, substantial increases in personal wealth and disposable income over the last few decades, together with recent difficulties in other areas of investment and in the pensions industry, have combined to make this an ever-increasingly important area of personal financial planning.

There are many kinds of property investor. Some fall into it by accident, finding themselves with a second property through marriage, inheritance or other changes in personal circumstances.

Others move into property investment quite deliberately, seeing it as a safe haven providing long-term security. Still others use property investment as a means to generate a second income. Beyond these, there also lie the fields of property development, trading and management.

Most recently, a strong trend has emerged for people to enter the property business as a professional career. This "new breed" of property Investor is entering the market with a much higher degree of sophistication and is prepared to devote substantial time and resources to their business.

Despite the recent increase in interest rates and the media scrutiny of the self-certifying mortgage regime, I personally believe that the property investment sector as we know it today is here to stay. Naturally, the sector will have its ups and downs, as any other sector does, but the philosophy of property investment as a 'career move' is now so well entrenched that it has become impossible to imagine that it could ever disappear altogether.

Whatever reasons you may have for becoming a property investor, my aim in this guide is to both give you a better understanding of how the UK tax system affects property investment and provide you with some guidance on the techniques available to minimise or eliminate your potential tax liabilities.

In the first five chapters of the guide, I will concentrate on explaining how the UK tax rules apply to property investment and other types of property business. Whilst these earlier chapters do include plenty of tax planning tips, it is in chapter six that I will examine some of the most popular and useful planning strategies which you the investor can employ to reduce your tax burden.

I believe that this guide is now comprehensive enough to meet the needs of almost every UK property investor and I hope that, with the help of this guide, you will be able to enjoy a much larger proportion of the fruits of your endeavours.

Finally, I would just like to thank you for buying this guide and wish you every success with your property investments.

Scope of this Guide

In this guide, we aim to cover as much as possible of the UK tax implications of investing in property. There are three different types of property investor for whom UK tax will be an issue. These three types of investor may be summarised as follows:

i)   UK residents investing in UK property.
ii)   UK residents investing in overseas property.
iii)   Non-UK residents investing in UK property.

Obviously, the same person might have investments falling under both (i) and (ii) and we will cater for that situation also.

For tax purposes, the UK does not include the Channel Islands or the Isle of Man.

Wealth Warning

It is important to remember that both UK residents investing in property overseas and non-UK residents investing in UK property may also face foreign tax liabilities on their property income and capital gains.

Each country has its own tax system and income or gains which are exempt in the UK may still be liable to tax elsewhere.

It is only where we are talking about UK residents investing in UK property that we can be absolutely certain that no other country has any right to tax the income or gains arising.

The tax planning strategies outlined in this guide are aimed primarily at UK resident investors. Non-UK residents face different issues, which are covered in further detail in the Taxcafe.co.uk guide to *Non Resident & Offshore Tax Planning.*

This guide is aimed primarily at those who are running a property business personally, jointly with another individual, or through a partnership. We will, however, also touch briefly on some of the issues arising when investing in property through other investment vehicles, such as limited companies, limited liability partnerships or property trusts. A great deal more detailed guidance on the implications of using a property company is contained in the Taxcafe.co.uk guide *Using a Property Company to Save Tax.*

Advice on these, or any other UK tax subjects, can be obtained through the Taxcafe.co.uk Question & Answer Service.

Finally, the reader must bear in mind the general nature of this guide. Individual circumstances vary and the tax implications of an individual's actions will vary with them.

Chapter 1

What is Property Tax?

1.1 Knowing Your Enemy

As already explained in the introduction, the first part of this guide is taken up with an explanation of how the UK tax system applies to property investment and other types of property business.

This is essential, because you cannot begin to consider how to avoid property tax until you actually understand what property tax is. In other words, you must "know your enemy" in order to be able to combat it most effectively.

The property investor needs to understand that there is no single "property tax", but rather a whole range of taxes which can apply to property. There is no point in avoiding one of these taxes only to find yourself paying even more in another! Horror stories of this nature happen all too frequently, such as the taxpayer who managed to avoid 1% Stamp Duty on part of his new house, only to find that he was stuck with a 17.5% VAT charge instead!

In this introductory chapter therefore, we will take a brief look at the taxes which can affect the property investor and give some consideration to the relative importance of each.

Later, when we begin to consider tax planning strategies, it is vital to bear in mind that it is the overall outcome which matters most, not simply saving or deferring any single type of tax.

1.2 What Taxes Face a Property Investor?

The only UK taxes which are specific to property are council tax (for residential property) and business rates (for commercial property) and these, in any case, are levied on the occupiers of property and not necessarily on the owners or investors.

However, the investor should not for a moment think this means that property investment gets off lightly under the UK tax system.

Far from it! Without the existence of any specific national tax, property investment is left exposed to a huge range of UK taxes. Tax is levied when property is purchased (Stamp Duty Land Tax), rented out (Income Tax) and sold (Capital Gains Tax). Property investors have to pay tax when they need to buy goods or services (VAT), when they make their investments through a company (Corporation Tax) and even when they die (Inheritance Tax).

When the successful investor needs to employ help in the business, he or she will have to pay PAYE and employer's National Insurance Contributions. Doubtless, they will also be paying Insurance Premium Tax, as well as Road Tax and duty on the petrol they buy as they travel in their business. They may even be paying air passenger duty if their business takes them far.

Faced with this horrifying list, investors might be excused for turning to drink, only to find themselves paying yet more tax!

1.3 Which Taxes Are Most Important?

For most property investors, two taxes comprise the vast majority of the actual or potential tax burden which they will face during their lifetime. These are Income Tax and Capital Gains Tax and they are covered in detail in Chapters three and four respectively.

The exact way in which these two very important taxes will actually be applied to your property business will depend on exactly what type of property investor you are. For tax purposes, there are a number of different categories into which a property business might fall and it is crucial that you understand how your business is likely to be classified before you can attempt to plan your tax affairs. I will return to this question in more detail in chapter two.

Other taxes which may also have a significant impact include Stamp Duty Land Tax, Inheritance Tax, VAT and National Insurance, and these are covered in Chapter five.

For those investors using a company, Corporation Tax will become of equal, if not greater, importance to the two main taxes.

1.4 How Does Property Tax Compare with Tax on Other Types of Income?

At present, property income could reasonably be described as "middle-ranking" in terms of the level of tax which is levied on it in the UK.

On the one hand, property income is treated less favourably than:

a) Dividends – basic rate taxpayers have no liability on UK dividends and higher rate taxpayers suffer an effective rate of only 25%.

b) Other savings income (primarily interest) – basic rate taxpayers pay 20% rather than 22%.

On the other hand, however, one saving grace is that property rental income is not regarded as "earnings". In the past, when we had the "unearned income surcharge", this would have been quite disadvantageous.

Now though, as explained in section 5.6, it means that most property income does not generally give rise to any liability for National Insurance Contributions.

This means that the effective tax burden on income received is much less than for:

a) Self-employment or partnership trading income – most taxpayers have to pay an additional 8% in Class 4 National Insurance Contributions on the majority of their profits, plus £2.05 a week in Class 2 National Insurance Contributions.

b) Employment income – the combined National Insurance Contributions burden for employers and employees on most earnings is 23.8%.

Note, however, that if your property business is classed as a trade, you will be subject to Class 2 and 4 NIC.

1.5 What About Capital Taxes?

Unfortunately, this is where property investment really can suffer in comparison to other forms of investment.

The rates of Stamp Duty Land Tax on property are now quite prohibitive (see section 5.2), especially when compared with the single 0.5% rate of Stamp Duty which still applies to shares and securities.

Capital Gains Tax is extremely complex, as we will see in Chapter four. Whilst the tax has a highly complicated system of reliefs and exemptions, which can work well for the wiser and better prepared property investor, it is nevertheless somewhat disappointing to note that the most popular forms of property investment will fail to attract the more advantageous Business Asset Taper Relief (see section 4.16).

Finally (in more ways than one), there is the fact that Inheritance Tax will most likely be payable in full on most property investments if the investor fails to plan effectively during his or her lifetime.

Dealing with the Inland Revenue

At various points in this guide, you will see me refer to your "Tax Office". This is the Inland Revenue office that sends you your tax return or, if you are not yet in the self-assessment system, the office that your employer deals with. Failing either of these, it will be the local Inland Revenue office for the area where you live and can be found in the telephone directory under "Inland Revenue".

Chapter 2

What Kind of Property Investor Are You?

2.1 Introduction

Before we begin to look in detail at exactly how property businesses are taxed in the UK, we must first consider what type of property business we are looking at. This is an essential step, as the tax treatment of a property business will vary according to the type of business activities involved.

While it would be possible to come up with a very long list of different 'types' of property business, I would tend to regard the following four categories as the definitive list as far as UK taxation treatment is concerned:

- a) Property investment (or letting)
- b) Property development
- c) Property trading (or dealing)
- d) Property management

Before we go on to look at the detailed tax treatment of these different types of property business, it is perhaps worth spending a little time to explain exactly what these different terms mean in a taxation context.

It is also important to understand that these different types of property business are not exclusive to individual property investors and that these different categorisations may also be applied to a property company, a partnership, or any other kind of property investment vehicle.

The reason we need to consider these different types of property business here is the fact that an understanding of what type of property business you have is crucial in determining which taxes will apply to your business and when.

A property investor may, of course, be carrying on more than one type of property business, which would result in a mixture of tax treatments. I will spend a little time on the possible consequences of this in section 2.6.

2.2 Property Investment (or Property Letting)

These are businesses that predominantly hold properties as long-term investments. The properties are the business's fixed assets, which are held to produce income in the form of rental profit.

While capital growth will be anticipated and will form part of the investor's business plan, property disposals should usually only take place where there is a strong commercial reason, such as an anticipated decline in value in that particular geographical location or a need to realise funds for other investments.

In general, properties will be held for a long period and rapid sales for short-term gain will be exceptional. Having said that, where unexpected opportunities for short-term gains do arise, it would be unreasonable to suggest that the investor should not make the most of them.

It is symptomatic of any property investment business that the investor has a minimal level of involvement in the day-to-day business. The majority of buy-to-let investors would be regarded as having this type of business.

Example
Fletcher purchases three properties 'off-plan' in September 2004. On completion of the properties in January 2005, he sells one of them in order to provide funds for further purchases. The other two properties are then rented out for a number of years.

Although Fletcher sold one of the properties very quickly, there was a good commercial reason for doing so. Hence, he may still be regarded as having a property investment business.

Tax Treatment

An investor with a property investment business must account for his rental profits under the specific rules applying to income from land and property (see sections 3.6 to 3.17).

Property disposals are dealt with as capital gains.

Is there any advantage to being regarded as having a property investment business rather than one of the other types of property business?

Yes, there is often quite an advantage for an individual property investor (or a partnership, trust, etc.) in having a property investment business instead of one of the other types of property business.

This is because of the fact that property disposals are treated as capital gains, taxed under the Capital Gains Tax regime and not income which is taxed under the Income Tax regime.

This, in turn, provides the investor with the opportunity to make the most of the many different reliefs available within the Capital Gains Tax regime (see Chapter four).

> **Tax Tip**
>
> For a non-UK Resident investor, capital gains are completely exempt from UK Capital Gains Tax. For these investors, treatment as a property investment business rather than any other type of property business is therefore an enormous advantage and they would be well advised to take care to arrange their affairs accordingly.

It is always important to remember that it is the way in which you carry on your business which determines the treatment, it is not a matter of choice!

2.3 Property Development

These are businesses which predominantly acquire properties or land and carry out building or renovation work with a view to selling developed properties for profit.

The term covers quite a broad spectrum of activities, from major building companies that acquire vacant land and construct vast new property developments, to casual property investors who acquire the occasional 'run-down' property to 'do up' for onward sale at a profit. No one will doubt that the former are correctly categorised as property developers, but not everyone realises that the latter type of activity will also lead to the investors being regarded as property developers.

Generally speaking, a property will be disposed of as soon as possible after building or renovation work has been completed. It is the profit derived from this work that produces the business's income and the owners do not usually look to rent properties out other than as a matter of short-term expediency.

Example
Godber purchases three old barns in February 2005 and converts them into residential property. The work is completed in August 2005 and he then sells two of the former barns immediately.

The third barn, unfortunately, proves difficult to sell. In order to generate some income from the property, Godber lets it out on a short six-month lease. The property is never taken off the market during the period of the lease and a buyer is found in January 2006, with completion taking place in March.

Although Godber let one of the properties out for a short period, his main business activity remained property development. This was reinforced by the fact that the property had remained on the market throughout the lease. Godber therefore has a property development business.

Tax Treatment

A property development business is regarded as a trade.

The profits from property development activities, i.e. the profits arising from development property sales, are taxed as trading profits. Trading profits are subject to both Income Tax and National Insurance (see further in sections 3.18 and 5.6).

Where, as in the example above, there is some incidental short-term rental income it should, strictly speaking, still be dealt with under the specific rules applying to income from land and property. In practice, however, it has sometimes been known for this to be accepted as incidental trading income.

The great disadvantage of being a property developer is the fact that all profits are dealt with under the Income Tax regime and not the Capital Gains Tax regime. This means that reliefs such as the annual Capital Gains Tax exemption, principal private residence relief and private letting relief will not be available.

On the other hand, however, the business itself, if it has any value (e.g. Goodwill), will attract Business Asset Taper Relief and Business Property Relief for Inheritance Tax purposes.

Capital gains treatment will continue to apply to any disposals of the business's long-term fixed assets, such as its own offices, for example.

Larger property development businesses, which utilise the services of sub-contractors, are required to operate the Construction Industry Scheme for tax purposes. Broadly, this involves having to deduct tax, at a special rate particular to the Construction Industry Scheme, from payments made to sub-contractors and then account for it to the Inland Revenue, rather like PAYE.

2.4 Property Trading

This type of property business is fairly rare. A property trader generally only holds properties for short-term gain. Properties are bought and sold frequently and are held as trading stock. Such traders may sometimes also be known as property dealers.

Properties will not usually be rented out, except for short-term financial expediency.

These investors derive their income simply by making a profit on the properties they sell.

Property traders differ from property developers in that no actual development takes place on the properties. Profits are made simply by ensuring a good margin between buying price and selling price.

Example
Mr McKay buys 20 properties 'off-plan' in March 2005. On completion of the development in October 2005, he sells all 20 properties at a considerable profit.

Since Mr McKay has neither developed the properties, nor held on to them as investments for any length of time, he is clearly a property trader.

Tax Treatment

A property trader's profits from property sales should be taxed as trading profits within the Income Tax regime. Once again, these profits are also subject to National Insurance Contributions (see section 5.6).

As with a property developer, any incidental letting income that does arise should be dealt with under the specific rules applying to income from land and property.

The value of this type of business is specifically not eligible for Business Property Relief for Inheritance Tax purposes.

As for Capital Gains Tax taper relief, the theory is that a property trading business is still a 'trade' and hence the long-term assets of such a business (e.g. goodwill or office premises) should be eligible for the faster 'business asset' taper relief. In practice, however, I feel that there is a strong danger that some resistance will be encountered, with the Inland Revenue contending that the business is, in fact, a property investment business and hence its long-term assets do not qualify as 'business assets'. Time will tell on this one!

Wealth Warning

The major difference between property investment and property trading lies in the treatment of the profit arising on property disposals. In essence, the question is whether such 'profits' are capital gains or trading profits.

This is very much a 'grey area' and hence the Inland Revenue can be expected to examine borderline cases very carefully and to argue for the treatment that produces the most tax.

As explained above, the Inland Revenue may be inclined to deny the existence of a trading activity where taper relief is at stake.

Conversely, where an investor is potentially exempt from Capital Gains Tax (e.g. a non-resident) on capital gains, the Inland Revenue may argue that there is a trading activity in order to be able to levy Income Tax on that investor instead. (Assuming that we are talking about a UK property business.)

A property company may be useful in this latter case, as there is less difference in the amount of tax payable *within* a company between a property 'trading' business or a property 'investment' business. Although this does effectively mean 'admitting defeat' and accepting that the business will be taxable in the UK, it is nevertheless a case of 'damage limitation' as the Corporation Tax rates applying will generally be lower than the Income Tax which is potentially at stake.

2.5 Property Management

These businesses do not generally own properties at all. Instead, they provide management services to property owners. If you have a property letting agent taking care of the day-to-day running of your properties, the chances are that it is probably a property management company.

A property management business's income is derived from the management or service charges it charges to the actual owners of the property.

Tax Treatment

A property management business is a trade for all tax purposes.

The long-term assets of a property management business are usually regarded as business assets for both Capital Gains Tax taper relief and Inheritance Tax purposes.

The profits arising from property management activities will be treated as trading profits, subject to both Income Tax and National Insurance Contributions.

Any incidental letting income should, as usual, be dealt with under the specific rules applying to income from land and property.

2.6 'Mixed' Property Businesses

"What if my business doesn't happen to fit neatly into one of these four categories?" you may be asking.

If you have a 'mixed' property business, involving more than one of the four types of property business described above, to a degree that is more than merely incidental, then, for tax purposes, each of the business types should be dealt with separately, in the usual manner applicable to that type.

However, having said that, there is a great danger that any property development or property trading may effectively "taint" what would otherwise be a property investment business, with the result that the Inland Revenue might attempt to deny you Capital Gains Tax treatment on all of your property transactions.

(Property management will generally stand alone without too much difficulty, as it does not involve any property ownership.)

Tax Tip

To avoid the danger of a property investment business being "tainted" by development or trading activities, you should take whatever steps you can to separate the businesses, such as:

i)   Drawing up separate accounts for the different businesses.
ii)   Using a different business name for the different activities.

iii)   Reporting the non-investment activities as a different business in your Tax Return.

iv)   Consider a different legal ownership structure for the non-investment activities (e.g. put them in a company or a partnership with your spouse or adult children).

Chapter 3

How to Avoid Income Tax

3.1 Introduction to Income Tax

Income tax will probably not be the first tax which you will encounter as a property investor. No, before you've even installed your first tenant you will most likely have had to pay some Stamp Duty Land Tax and some VAT on your legal and professional fees.

However, Income Tax is nevertheless still the first tax which causes the property investor any real concern and for this reason it seems appropriate to examine it first.

Income tax was originally introduced by William Pitt (the Younger) in 1799 as a "temporary measure" to enable the Government to raise the revenue required to fight the Napoleonic Wars. Bonaparte may have met his Waterloo in 1815, but it seems that the British taxpayer is still paying for it!

The tax was initially charged at a single rate of two shillings in the pound (10% in today's terms). The top rate rose to an all-time high of 95% under Harold Wilson's Labour Government of the 1960s. Rates remained fairly high (with a top rate of 60%) until Nigel Lawson's tax-cutting Budget of 1987 established the current higher rate of 40% as the top rate.

The long history of Income Tax may go some way towards explaining some of its quirks. Badly needed modernisation is often slow in coming. For example, it was only as recently as 1998 that "the expense of keeping a horse for the purposes of travel to the taxpayer's place of work" ceased to be allowable.

The roots of how Income Tax affects the property investor lie in the so-called "schedular" system of Income Tax introduced in the 19th Century. Under the schedular system, each type of income is classified separately and taxed under a different "Schedule". Since 1970, income from land and property has been designated as Schedule A (except in those cases which represent trading income, which falls under Schedule D Case I).

The rules governing rental income under Schedule A were, until relatively recently, somewhat archaic and hence rather restrictive. Fortunately, however, in 1995 the system underwent something of an overhaul producing the rather more sensible rules we have today which, quite rightly, treat property investment as a business. (But not usually as a trade, as we will see to our frustration later in this guide.)

Other major changes in recent years have included the introduction of "separate taxation" for husbands and wives in 1990 (before which a wife's "unearned" income was treated as her husband's for tax purposes) and, of course, self assessment, which came into force from 6th April 1996.

However, despite recent reforms, Income Tax has passed its bicentenary with some of its greatest peculiarities still intact. Rumours of a possible merger of Income Tax and National Insurance Contributions have, thankfully for property investors (see section 5.6), so far come to nothing. And the greatest oddity of all, the UK's peculiar tax year-end date of 5th April has survived into the 21st Century. But how long can it be before pressure from the European Union forces the UK, like the Irish Republic, to adopt a calendar year?

3.2 Basic Principles of Income Tax

The UK tax year runs from 6th April each year to the following 5th April. The year ending 5th April 2005 is referred to as "2004/2005" and the tax return for this year is known as the "2005 Return".

Since 1996/1997, individuals and trusts have been subject to the self-assessment system for UK Income Tax.

Under this system, the taxpayer must complete and submit a tax return by 31st January following each tax year. The taxpayer must also calculate the amount of tax he or she is due to pay, although the Inland Revenue will do the calculation themselves if the return reaches them by 30th September following the tax year.

The Income Tax due under the self-assessment system is basically the taxpayer's total tax liability for the year less any amounts already deducted at source or under PAYE and less any applicable tax credits.

All Income Tax due under the self assessment system, regardless of the source of the income or rate of tax applying is payable as follows:

- A first instalment or "payment on account" is due on 31st January during the tax year.
- A second payment on account is due on 31st July following the tax year.
- A balancing payment or, in some cases, a repayment, is due on 31st January following the tax year.

Each payment on account is usually equal to half of the previous tax year's self assessment tax liability. However, payments on account need not be made when the previous year's self assessment liability was either:

a) No more than £500, or
b) Less than 20% of the taxpayer's total tax liability for the year.

Additionally, applications to reduce payments on account may be made when there are reasonable grounds to believe that the following year's self assessment tax liability will be at a lower level.

Taxpayers who are in employment or in receipt of pensions (other than state pensions) may apply to have self-assessment tax liabilities which do not exceed £2,000 collected through their PAYE codes for the following tax year. This produces a considerable cashflow advantage, where relevant. Tax returns must be submitted by 30th September following the tax year if taxpayers wish to make such an application. (E.g. submit tax return for the tax year ending 5th April 2004 (2003/2004) by 30th September 2004 to claim to have up to £2,000 collected through PAYE coding for 2005/2006.)

The self assessment system, as described above, is also used to collect Class 4 National Insurance Contributions on self-employed or partnership trading income and certain student loan repayments.

3.3 Rates of Tax

The current UK Income Tax rates and main allowances are set out in Appendix A.

Income from land and property forms part of the "non-savings" or "other" element of a taxpayer's income and is therefore currently taxed at three rates, namely 10%, 22% and 40%.

These same rates also apply to any trading income arising from property development, trading or management.

3.4 Calculating the Income Tax Due

The best way to explain how Income Tax due under self assessment is calculated is by way of an example.

In this example, we will look at the "before" and "after" scenarios applying to a taxpayer who begins to receive rental profits. The example will also demonstrate the impact that beginning to receive untaxed income, such as rental profits, may have on the timing of an individual's tax liabilities.

Furthermore, this example will illustrate the effect of an anomaly which is caused by the way in which different types of income are now taxed at different rates. As so-called "other" income, property income is taxed before "savings" income such as interest or dividends. This means that the ability to benefit from the lower rates applying to these types of income may be lost when the taxpayer begins to receive property income. This, in turn, can sometimes create an effective tax rate of 42% on the additional income.

Example – Part 1 (Basic Income Tax Calculation, or "Before")

In the tax year 2004/2005, Nick receives a gross salary of £20,000 and gross interest income of £18,000. He has already suffered Income Tax deductions totalling £3,113.70 under PAYE on his salary as well as Income Tax deducted at source on his interest of £3,600.

His self assessment tax liability for the year is calculated as follows:

Employment Income:	£20,000	
Less: Personal Allowance:	(£4,745)	
Total "Other" Income Taxable:	£15,255	
Income Tax @ 10% on £2,020:		£202.00
Income Tax @ 22% on balance (£13,235):		£2,911.70
Interest Income:	£18,000	

Income Tax @ 20% on remainder of basic rate band
(£16,145 = £29,380 LESS £13,235 already used) £3,229.00
Income Tax @ 40% on balance (£1,855): £742.00

Total Tax For The Year: £7,084.70

Less: Tax paid under PAYE £3,113.70
Tax deducted at source from interest £3,600.00
  £6,713.70

Tax due under self assessment £371.00

Nick can either pay this tax directly to the Inland Revenue in one single lump sum (due by 31st January 2006) or, if he submits his 2005 tax return by 30th September, apply to have it collected through his PAYE coding for 2006/2007.

Nick's tax liability is too small for him to be required to make any payments on account in respect of his 2005/2006 tax liability.

Example – Part 2 (Introducing Rental Income, or "After")

In addition to his salary and interest income, Nick also has rental profits of £10,000. His Income Tax calculation for 2004/2005 now proceeds as follows:

Employment Income:	£20,000	
Income from Land and Property:	£10,000	
Less: Personal Allowance:	(£4,745)	
Total "Other" Income Taxable:		£25,255

Income Tax @ 10% on £2,020:		£202.00
Income Tax @ 22% on balance (£23,235):		£5,111.70

Interest Income:	£18,000	
Income Tax @ 20% on remainder of basic rate band		
(£6,145 = £29,380 LESS £23,235 already used):		£1,229.00
Income Tax @ 40% on balance (£11,855):		£4,742.00

Total Tax For The Year:	£11,284.70

Less: Tax paid under PAYE	£3,113.70	
Tax deducted at source from interest	£3,600.00	
		£6,713.70

Tax due under self assessment	£4,571.00

Immediately we can see that £10,000 of rental income has increased Nick's tax liability by £4,200 – hence producing the effective rate of 42% discussed above.

Although the rental income itself is only taxed at 22%, it also pushes an additional £10,000 of the interest income into the higher rate tax band, thus increasing the tax on that income from 20% to 40% - i.e. an extra 20%. The 42% effective rate is the sum of these two tax increases.

Not only does Nick have considerably more tax to pay, he is no longer eligible to pay his additional self-assessment tax liability through his PAYE coding and must also now make payments on account in respect of 2005/2006.

Hence, unless Nick has reasonable grounds for claiming that his 2005/2006 tax liability will be less than that for 2004/2005, he will have to make tax payments as follows:

- By 31st January 2006:
  Tax due for 2004/2005:   £4,571.00
  First Instalment for 2005/2006:   £2,285.50
  Total payment due: £6,856.50

- By 31st July 2006:
  Second Instalment for 2005/2006:   £2,285.50

- By 31st January 2007:
  Balancing payment (or repayment) for 2005/2006
  First Instalment for 2006/2007

- And so on, every six months thereafter.

The example has demonstrated a very important fact. When you begin to receive any significant level of untaxed income like rental profits, the tax liabilities arising in the first year can be quite severe. In effect, you will need to find the tax on two years' worth of profits within the space of only six months – most of it all on one single date. This is what I call the "double whammy" effect of self assessment!

Of course, once you are "in the system" and things settle down a bit, you should just be paying fairly similar levels of tax every six months. Nevertheless, every time your untaxed income increases significantly, you will be hit by this "double whammy" effect again!

Wealth Warning

Where a taxpayer is paying tax under both PAYE and Self-Assessment, (e.g. a property investor who is also in employment or has a private pension), the Inland Revenue have the power to collect the tax due on the taxpayer's untaxed income (e.g. rental income) through the PAYE system.

The Inland Revenue could deduct as much as 50% of a taxpayer's earnings directly at source through this mechanism.

The effect of this would be to vastly accelerate the collection of the tax due on rental income.

Whilst this power has existed for some time, it has very rarely been exercised in practice in recent years. Rumour has it, however, that the Inland Revenue may be looking to exercise this power more frequently in the near future.

Fortunately, at present, taxpayers have the right to appeal against any PAYE codings which attempt to include their rental income in this way and hence continue to pay the tax on their rental income via the self-assessment system.

3.5 Tax Returns

Rental income from UK land and property should be detailed on pages L1 and L2 of the tax return. This is referred to as the "Land and Property Supplement".

Income from the commercial letting of furnished holiday accommodation in the UK is treated in a special way for a number of tax purposes and is returned on page L1. Other UK property income should be dealt with on page L2.

Income from land and property located overseas is treated as a different source of income and should be detailed on pages F4 and F5 which form part of the "Foreign Supplement".

Where your property business is deemed to be a "trade" for tax purposes, you will instead need to complete the "Self-Employment Supplement", pages SE1 to SE4.

If you have both investment and trading activities then you will need to complete both the Land and Property Supplement (and/or the Foreign Supplement, as appropriate) and the Self-Employment Supplement.

Where property is held jointly, each joint owner must include their own share of property income and expenses on their own tax return each year, as appropriate.

Tax return supplements can be obtained by calling the Revenue's own order line, 0845 9000 404 or by downloading them from www.inlandrevenue.gov.uk

Strictly speaking, whenever a taxpayer begins to receive income from a new source, they should advise the Inland Revenue of this new source by 5th October following the tax year in which it is first received. However, in practice, as long as the tax return includes the new source of income, and is completed and submitted by 31st January following the tax year, no penalties will arise. "New source" refers to the commencement of a UK property business or an overseas property business, rather than a new property within an existing property business.

In 2004, the Inland Revenue will be issuing approximately 400,000 new-style short returns. These new short returns will be only 4 pages long and will, in some circumstances, be able to detail all of a taxpayer's sources of income rather more concisely then the usual full tax return of 10 pages plus supplements.

Some property investors whose tax affairs are relatively simple will be receiving the new short return.

Wealth Warning

If you receive one of the new-style short returns, it remains your legal obligation to ensure that all of your income and capital gains are reported to the Inland Revenue, as appropriate.

In some cases, this will mean that you should revert to the normal full return and it is your responsibility to ascertain whether this is the case.

It is anticipated that the number of new-style short returns issued will increase to approximately 1,500,000 in 2005.

3.6 The Taxation of Rental Income Generally

Property letting is now treated very much like any other business for Income Tax purposes. You will need to draw up accounts which detail all your income as well as all relevant expenses.

If you are letting a number of UK properties on a commercial basis, this is treated as a single UK property business and one set of accounts will usually suffice (although many landlords prefer to have a separate set of accounts for each property).

Separate accounts, however, are required in the following cases:

- Furnished holiday lettings in the UK (see section 3.11).
- Overseas lettings (see section 3.15).
- Non-commercial lettings (see section 3.16).

All rental income must be included, no matter how modest the source, unless it is covered by the "Rent-A-Room" scheme (see section 3.12 below).

Unlike other types of business, however, you are not free to choose which accounting period you wish to use and must, instead, draw up accounts for the tax year, which runs from 6th April to the following 5th April.

Generally, your accounts have to be drawn up on an "accruals" basis. This means that income and expenditure is recognised when it arises, or is incurred, rather than when it is received or paid (the latter being the "cash basis" – see below). For example, if you started renting out a property on 12th March 2004, at a monthly rent of £1,000, the income you need to recognise in your accounts for the year ended 5th April 2004 is £1,000 x 12 x 25/366 = £819.67 (you are renting it for 25 days in the 2003/2004 tax year).

(Note here the minor, but possibly beneficial, point that 2003/2004 is a "leap tax year" of 366 days duration.)

Expenses may similarly be recognised as they are incurred. For example, if you have some roof repairs carried out on a rented property in March 2004, you may deduct the cost in your accounts to 5th April 2004, even if the roofer doesn't invoice you until May.

Concessionary Use of Cash Basis

By concession, the Inland Revenue will still allow taxpayers whose gross annual receipts do not exceed £15,000 to use the old "cash basis". As stated above, this means that income and expenditure may be recognised when received or paid. The Revenue will only allow this method to be used where it is applied consistently and produces a reasonable result not substantially different from that produced on the usual accruals basis.

In most cases, since rent is usually received in advance and expenses are often paid in arrears, the cash basis will not be beneficial. Nevertheless, when you are starting out with a relatively modest level of rental income, it is an option to consider.

3.7 Deductible Expenditure

The rules on what types of expenditure may be claimed as deductions are much the same as for other types of business. Some of the main deductions include:

- Interest and other finance costs (covered in further detail in section 3.8 below)
- Property maintenance and repair costs
- Heating and lighting costs, if borne by the landlord
- Insurance costs
- Letting agent's fees
- Advertising for tenants
- Accountancy fees
- Legal and professional fees (see further below)
- The cost of cleaners, gardeners, etc, where relevant
- Ground rent, service charges, etc.
- Bad debts
- Pre-trading expenditure (see further below)
- Landlord's administrative expenditure (see further below)

All expenses must be incurred wholly and exclusively for the purposes of the property business and, naturally, must actually be borne by the taxpayer themselves (i.e. you cannot claim any expenses if your tenant is paying them directly).

The term "wholly and exclusively" is enshrined in tax law but it is not always interpreted quite as literally as you might think.

Example

Gregor pays £50 per week for gardening services. This covers the upkeep of his own garden and that of the house next door, which he also owns and rents out.

This is what we call "mixed use". The gardening costs are partly private expenditure and partly incurred for Gregor's property business. This does not mean that all of the gardening expenditure falls foul of the "wholly and exclusively" rule. The correct interpretation is to say that part of the gardening expenses are incurred wholly and exclusively for business purposes and to claim an appropriate proportion.

Legal and Professional Fees

Legal fees and other professional costs incurred for the purposes of the business may be claimed as a deduction against rental income. Typically, this will include items such as the costs of preparing tenants' leases and, perhaps, debt collection expenses.

Legal fees and other costs incurred on the purchase or sale of properties, however, may not usually be claimed for Income Tax purposes (unless you are trading as a property developer). All is not lost though, as these items may be claimed as allowable deductions for Capital Gains Tax purposes (see Chapter Four).

Pre-Trading Expenditure

You may incur some expenses for the purposes of your property business before you even start to let any properties out. Such expenses incurred within seven years before the commencement of your business may still be allowable if they would otherwise qualify under normal principles. In such cases, the expenses may be claimed as if they were incurred on the first day of the business.

Landlord's Administrative Expenditure

This heading is perhaps the broadest, and can extend to the cost of running an office, motor and travel costs and support staff's wages. As usual, the rule is that any expenditure must be incurred wholly and exclusively for the purposes of the business. Sadly though, any entertaining expenditure is specifically excluded.

31

3.8 Interest and Other Finance Costs

Interest is allowable if it is incurred for the purposes of the property business. Hence, the question of whether the interest on a loan is an allowable deduction is based on the use to which the funds borrowed were put. It does not, as many people seem to think, depend on which property the loan is secured on.

Interest Example 1

Matthew takes out a buy-to-let mortgage on a house which he begins to let out. This is the most usual and simple situation and, naturally, Matthew may claim the interest on his buy-to-let mortgage against his rental income from the house.

Interest Example 2

Mark takes out a personal loan and spends the funds on making improvements to a flat which he subsequently lets out. The interest on his loan is deductible because it has been incurred for the purpose of his property business.

Interest Example 3

Luke re-finances one of his rental properties and obtains additional funds of £10,000 in the process. He spends this money by taking his wife on a luxury cruise. The interest on Luke's additional borrowings are not deductible against his rental income as the funds were not used for business purposes.

Summary

In summary, interest will be allowable if it arises on funds borrowed to purchase or improve rental properties or otherwise expended for the purposes of the property business.

A last point to note is that interest on borrowings used to finance the purchase or improvement of a property will generally cease to be allowable if that property ceases to be used in the rental business (e.g. if it is subsequently adopted as the taxpayer's own residence).

Other Finance Costs

The treatment of other finance costs, such as loan arrangement fees, will generally follow the same principles as that for interest. In other words, the key factor will always be the purpose to which the borrowed funds are put.

Difficulties may sometimes occur, however, over the timing of relief for such costs. Sometimes, general accounting principles may dictate that the cost should be spread over the life of the loan. In such cases, the tax treatment will follow the same principles.

Early redemption fees will usually be regarded as a personal cost rather than a business cost and hence will neither be allowable for Income Tax nor for Capital Gains Tax. However, an Income Tax claim might be possible under general principles where there is a business reason for the early redemption.

3.9 Capital Expenditure

The main types of disallowable expenditure are capital expenditure on property improvements and on furniture, fixtures and fittings. There are special rules for capital expenditure, depending on the type of property being rented:

a) So-called "industrial property" attracts capital allowances on the cost of the building itself. These allowances are at the rate of 4% of cost per annum, but usually only apply to large structures, such as factories and warehouses, although they can also extend to garage workshops, for example.

b) Other commercial property, such as shops, offices etc, do not attract any allowances on the structure. However, any fixtures and fittings provided by the landlord in non-residential property do attract allowances. These allowances are more generous, up to 50% of cost being allowed in the first year (depending on the size of your business – see below) and 25% per annum of the unrelieved balance thereafter.

c) Residential property does not usually attract any capital allowances at all. However, landlords may claim a "wear

d) and tear allowance" (see section 3.10 below) on furnished lettings.

e) Furnished holiday lettings (see section 3.11 below), however, are not eligible for the wear and tear allowance, but are eligible for capital allowances in the same way as (b) above.

Capital allowances claimed previously may be reclaimed by the Revenue, i.e. added back on to income (known as a "balancing charge") when the property is sold.

The allowance of up to 50% under (b) above is only available for small businesses incurring capital expenditure during the tax year 2004/2005. From 6th April 2005, this rate will revert to 40%, in line with that available for "medium-sized" businesses.

"Small" and "Medium-Sized" for these purposes are as defined under Company Law. Broadly speaking, a business is "Small" if it meets at least two of the following three tests:

i)   Turnover (i.e. gross income) does not exceed £5,600,000 per annum.
ii)   Total asset value does not exceed £2,800,000.
iii)   It has no more than 50 employees.

Most property businesses will tend to qualify as "Small" on the basis that they meet tests (i) and (iii).

A "Medium-Sized" business is one which fails to meet the "Small" business test but which does meet at least two out of the following three tests:

i)   Turnover (i.e. gross income) does not exceed £22,800,000 per annum.
ii)   Total asset value does not exceed £11,400,000.
iii)   It has no more than 250 employees.

Insulation Costs

From 6th April 2004, landlords will be able to claim an Income Tax deduction for up to £1,500 of expenditure on new loft or cavity wall insulation. Previously, this would have been regarded as a capital item and hence disallowed.

3.10 Furnished Lettings

Income from furnished lettings (other than furnished holiday lettings, as defined – see section 3.11 below) is treated in much the same way as other rental income. The only differences, quite naturally, being related to the treatment of the furnishings.

No allowance is given for the initial expenditure in furnishing the property. Thereafter, the landlord may claim either:

> a) Renewal and replacement expenditure, or

> b) The "wear and tear allowance"

The Wear & Tear Allowance

A "Wear and Tear Allowance" of 10% of net rents receivable may be claimed against the rental income from furnished residential lettings. This Allowance is given instead of Capital Allowances, which are not available, and as an alternative to the "Replacements Basis".

In calculating the Allowance, we first need to establish the amount of "net rents receivable" for the property in question.

"Net rents receivable" means the total rent receivable less any amounts borne by the landlord which would normally be a tenant's own responsibility (e.g. council tax, water rates or electricity charges).

Additionally, if the rental includes any material amount representing a payment for additional services which would normally be borne by the occupier, rather than the owner, of the property, then these amounts must also be deducted before calculating the 10% Allowance.

Example

Cherie owns a large flat in central Bristol which she lets out for £2,500 per month (£30,000 per annum). This includes a charge of £250 per month for the provision of a cleaner. Cherie also pays the water rates for the property, which amount to £1,000 per year, but the tenant pays their own council tax.

She is therefore able to claim a wear and tear allowance as follows:

Total Rent Received:	*£30,000*
Less:	
Cleaning charges:	*£3,000 (12 x £250)*
Water Rates	*£1,000*
Net rent receivable:	*£26,000*
Wear and Tear Allowance:	*£2,600 (10%)*

Note that whilst we only have to deduct the COST of the water rates, it is the amount which Cherie CHARGES for the provision of cleaning services which must be deducted in this calculation. (Although only the cost thereof can be deducted when arriving at Cherie's overall total rental profits.)

The Alternative: The "Replacements Basis"

The Wear and Tear Allowance is not mandatory. Landlords may, instead, claim the cost of repairing, replacing or renewing furniture and fixtures. They may not, however, claim the costs of the original furnishings and fixtures when the property is first let out, nor the cost of improvements or additional items.

For example, replacing one Video Recorder with another (lucky tenants!) would be allowed under the Replacements Basis, but replacing a Video Recorder with a DVD Player (even luckier tenants!) would not, as it would represent an improvement.

The "Catch"

The Wear and Tear Allowance and the Replacements Basis are alternatives. You may claim one OR the other, NOT both.

However, building repair costs continue to be allowable under both methods and this extends to repairs and replacements of any items normally provided in an unfurnished property, such as sinks or toilets, for example

The "BIG" Catch

Once you have chosen one method, you must stick with it, on ALL of your furnished lets of all properties!

Hence, once the wear and tear allowance has been claimed, no deductions can ever be claimed for any repairs or renewals of furniture, fixtures, etc.

Tax Tip

If you were considering acquiring two or more properties and did have a clear idea that the wear and tear allowance was best for one (or more) of them, but the replacements basis would be better for the rest, you could consider acquiring the "wear and tear" properties personally, whilst your spouse (or perhaps a trust or partnership) could acquire the others and elect for the replacements basis.

So, Which Method Is Best?

Conventional wisdom states that the Wear and Tear Allowance is usually best. This is generally because this method provides some relief immediately, from the first year onwards.

Generally, it will take longer before replacement expenditure starts to come through, with the original capital cost of furnishings being unallowable.

In short, Wear and Tear generally provides faster relief.

However, it is worth bearing in mind that this will not always be the case.

Example 2

Tony rents out a number of small flats to students at the local Polytechnic (sorry, it's called a UNIVERSITY now).

He is constantly frustrated by the fact that they frequently wreck the furniture. However, he combats this by buying cheap furniture and keeping their security deposits.

As a result, his total rental income for 2004/2005 is £20,000. Out of this he has paid Council Tax and Water Rates totalling £2,000 and spent £3,000 on replacement furniture.

If Tony were to claim the Wear and Tear Allowance, he would only be able to deduct £1,800 from his rental income. Hence, he is much better off claiming £3,000 under the Replacement Basis.

(With apologies to all those students who treat their landlord's property with the utmost respect and to any student landlords who do not buy cheap furniture or look for any excuse to hang on to their security deposits.)

So How Do You Choose?

Despite Tony's example, most people are better off with the Wear and Tear Allowance. However, before you submit your first claim, I would suggest you do a few quick calculations to see which method is likely to be better for you on average in the long run (and not just in the first year).

3.11 Furnished Holiday Lettings

UK properties qualifying as "furnished holiday lettings" enjoy a special tax regime, with many of the tax advantages usually only accorded to a trade.

Many of the additional reliefs available for this type of property are discussed elsewhere in this guide. However, it is worth us taking a brief look at the qualification requirements:

i) The property must be situated in the UK.
ii) The property must be furnished (although there is no stipulation regarding the standard to which it must be furnished).
iii) It must be let out on a commercial basis with a view to the realisation of profits.
iv) It must be available for commercial letting to the public generally for at least 140 days in a twelve month period.
v) It must be so let for at least 70 such days.

vi) The property must not normally be in the same occupation for more than 31 consecutive days at any time during a period of at least seven months out of the same twelve month period as that referred to in (iii) above.

The twelve month period referred to in (iv) and (vi) above is normally the tax year, but special rules apply for the years in which letting commences or ceases. A system of averaging may be used to determine whether a taxpayer with more than one property meets (v) above. This requires a claim by the taxpayer.

3.12 Rent a Room Relief

A special relief, called "rent-a-room relief", applies to income from letting out a part of your own home. For this purpose, the property must be your only or main residence (see section 4.11) for at least part of the same tax year. The letting itself must also at least partially coincide with a period when the property is your main residence.

The relief covers not only income from lodgers, but also extends to the letting of a self-contained flat, provided that the division of the property is only temporary.

3.12.1 Complete Exemption

Complete exemption is automatically provided where the gross rent receivable from lettings in the property does not exceed the rent-a-room limit (currently £4,250). This limit is applied on an annual basis.

The taxpayer may elect not to claim rent-a-room relief if desired. They might do this, for example, if the letting is actually producing a loss which, otherwise, could not be claimed (see section 3.13 below regarding losses).

This election must be made before the expiry of a period ending twelve months after the 31st January following the tax year. (Eg for the tax year 2003/2004, such an election would need to be made by 31st January 2006).

3.12.2 Partial Exemption

Where the gross rent receivable exceeds the rent-a-room limit the taxpayer may nevertheless elect, (within the same time limit as outlined in 3.12.1 above), for a form of partial exemption.

The partial exemption operates by allowing the taxpayer to be assessed only on the amount of gross rents receivable in excess of the rent-a-room limit instead of under the normal basis for rental income (as outlined in section 3.6 above).

Example

Duncan rents out a room in his house for an annual rent of £5,000. His rental profit for 2003/2004, calculated on the normal basis, is £1,800. He therefore elects to use the rent-a-room basis, thus reducing his assessable rental income to only £750.

3.12.3 Other Points on Rent-a-Room Relief

Where the letting income is being shared with another person, the rent-a-room limit must be halved.

Where there is letting income from the same property during the same tax year which does not qualify for the relief, none of the income from the property that year may be exempted.

An election to claim rent-a-room relief is deemed to remain in place for future years unless withdrawn (the same time limit applies for a withdrawal).

Any balancing charges arising in the tax year (see section 3.9 above) must be added to gross rents receivable before considering the application of the rent-a-room relief limit.

3.12.4 A Final Point On Lodgers

Income from lodgers can sometimes be regarded as trading income where there are sufficient services being provided (cooking, cleaning, etc.). The rent-a-room relief still applies to this income in the same way however, it is only the treatment of any excess which would differ.

3.13 Rental Losses

As explained in section 3.6, all your UK property lettings (including any furnished holiday lettings) are treated as a single UK property business. Hence, the loss on any one such property is automatically set off against profits on other commercially let UK properties for the same period.

Any overall net losses arising from a UK property business may be carried forward and set off against future UK rental profits. Losses consisting of capital allowances may also be set off against the landlord's other income of the same tax year and the next one.

Any losses from UK furnished holiday lettings may additionally be set off against all of the taxpayer's other income of the same tax year and the previous one.

The treatment of losses from overseas lettings is covered in section 3.15 below. Non-commercial lettings are covered in section 3.16.

3.14 Other Property Income

Any form of income derived from property will generally be subject to Income Tax.

In particular, premiums received for the granting of short leases of no more than 50 years' duration are subject to Income Tax.

The proportion of the premium subject to Income Tax is, however, reduced by 2% for each full year of the lease's duration in excess of one year.

The element of the lease not subject to Income Tax falls within the Capital Gains Tax regime (see section 4.25) and will be treated as a part disposal of the relevant property (or superior interest).

Example 3.14.1

Alexander, who owns the freehold to a property, grants a 12-year lease to Kenneth for a premium of £50,000.

The lease exceeds one year by 11 years and hence 22% of this sum falls within the Capital Gains Tax regime. Alexander is therefore subject to Income Tax on the sum of £39,000 (i.e. £50,000 less 22%).

3.15 Overseas Lettings

All of a taxpayer's commercial overseas lettings are treated as a single business in much the same way as, but separate from, a UK property business. A UK resident and domiciled taxpayer (see section 3.17) with overseas lettings is taxed on this income under exactly the same principles as for UK lettings except that:

- Separate accounts will be required for properties in each overseas territory where any double tax relief claims are to be made.
- Overseas furnished holiday lettings are not eligible for any of the extra reliefs accorded to UK furnished holiday lettings.

Travelling expenses may be claimed when incurred wholly and exclusively for the purposes of the overseas letting business.

The UK treatment of losses arising from an overseas letting business is exactly the same as for a UK property business, except, of course, that this is treated as a separate business from any UK lettings which the taxpayer has. Hence, again, these losses are automatically set off against profits derived from other overseas lettings with the excess carried forward for set off against future overseas rental profits. The same rule as set out in section 3.13 applies to any capital allowances but the additional reliefs for furnished holiday lettings are not available.

3.16 Non-Commercial Lettings

Where lettings are not on a commercial or "arm's length" basis, they cannot be regarded as part of the same UK or overseas property business as any commercial lettings which the taxpayer has. Profits remain taxable, but any losses arising may only be carried forward for set off against future profits from the same letting (i.e. the same property let to the same tenant).

Where the tenant of such a non-commercial letting is the previous owner of the property (e.g. a parent of the landlord), a new Income Tax charge will apply to the benefit so received by the tenant with effect from 6th April 2005.

3.17 Non-Residents, etc

Non-residents remain liable for UK Income Tax on property situated in the UK. They are not, however, liable for UK Income Tax on property situated abroad.

The taxation of non-residents will be subject to the terms of any double taxation agreement between the UK and their country of residence.

Certain classes of non-resident individuals with taxable income in the UK are entitled to the same personal allowances as UK residents (see Appendix A), and may set these off against that income. These include British and Commonwealth citizens, nationals of states within the European Economic Area (the European Union plus Norway, Iceland and Liechtenstein), Crown servants and residents of the Isle of Man or the Channel Islands.

UK residents who are also UK domiciled are liable for UK Income Tax on all worldwide income as it arises. UK resident but non-UK domiciled individuals, however, are only subject to UK Income Tax on income from property situated abroad as and when they remit it back to the UK (known as the "Remittance Basis").

The tax concepts of residence and domicile can sometimes be fairly complex and a full examination of them is beyond the scope of this guide. The only way to determine your residence or domicile for certain is to examine your own personal circumstances in detail. Broadly, though, in most cases:

- You are resident in the country in which you live.
- You are domiciled in the country where you were born or where your nationality lies.

Your residence can change throughout your life from year to year. Most people never change their domicile.

For the vast majority of people, the situation is quite straightforward and it is safe to say that, if you have British parents and have lived in the UK all of your life, then you are almost certainly UK resident and domiciled.

The concept of domicile is examined a little further in section 5.4.

On 9th April 2003, the Inland Revenue published a new consultation document on the taxation of non-UK resident and non-domiciled persons. This may eventually lead to some changes in the tax regime applying to these persons, although the timing and nature of any such changes cannot yet be predicted.

3.18 Trading Income

Where your property business is deemed to be a trade (see Chapter Two), you will be taxed under different principles to those outlined in many of the previous sections. Some of the differences arising have been highlighted already in this chapter. The other major differences to note are as follows:

i) You may choose a different accounting date and do not have to stick with a 5th April year end. This provides some tax planning opportunities, particularly in the early years of your business.

ii) You will be liable for Class 2 and Class 4 National Insurance Contributions (see section 5.6).

iii) Most legal and professional fees should be allowed as incurred, as an Income Tax deduction.

iv) A broader range of administrative expenditure will be claimable.

v) Capital allowances will be available only on your own business's long-term assets (as per part (b) in section 3.9).

vi) Properties will generally be held as trading stock. In most cases, all of your expenditure on the properties which you sell, including fixtures, fittings and furnishings, should be allowable deductions against your sale proceeds.

vii)   Trading losses may be set off against all of your other income and capital gains for the same tax year and the previous one.

viii)   The same trade may involve both properties in the UK and properties overseas.

ix)   Non-Resident individuals and non-domiciled individuals are taxed on a trade if it is managed in the UK. (For a UK Resident but non-domiciled individual, a foreign-based property trade is again taxed on the remittance basis.)

Chapter 4

How to Avoid Capital Gains Tax

4.1 The Importance of Capital Gains Tax

Although its impact is not as immediate as that of Income Tax, nevertheless Capital Gains Tax is perhaps the most significant tax from a property investor's perspective. Most property investments will eventually lead to a disposal and every property disposal presents the risk of a Capital Gains Tax liability arising and reducing the investor's after-tax return drastically, sometimes by as much as 40%.

Paradoxically, however, Capital Gains Tax is also the tax which presents the greatest number and variety of tax planning opportunities. We will be examining some of these further in Chapter Six. First, however, it is worth recalling how this tax developed and looking at how it affects property investors today.

4.2 The Development of Capital Gains Tax

Capital Gains Tax was introduced by Harold Wilson's first Labour Government in 1965. The new tax was designed to combat a growing trend for avoiding Income Tax by realising capital gains, which at that time were mostly tax free, rather than taxable income.

Because the tax was only introduced on 6th April 1965, gains arising before that date remained exempt from Capital Gains Tax and, for many years, it was thus necessary to make detailed, and often complicated, calculations designed to remove these "pre-1965" gains from the amount to be taxed. In theory, such calculations could still be relevant, although their incidence is now fairly rare.

The high inflation of the late 1970s and early 1980s brought about a significant change after 31st March 1982, with the introduction of Indexation Relief. This new relief was designed to exempt gains which arose purely through the effects of inflation. Ironically, and somewhat frustratingly, however, it was only post-March 1982 inflation which was exempted and, by then, the highest rates of inflation lay in the past.

The next major change came in 1988 with so-called "re-basing". The Government finally recognised the unfairness of not exempting pre-1982 inflationary gains. However, rather than merely combating this oversight with an improved Indexation Relief, instead they decided to exempt all pre-31st March 1982 gains. Hence Capital Gains Tax was "rebased" from 6th April 1965 to 31st March 1982.

Naturally, however, since nothing in the tax world is ever simple, the new 31st March 1982 base did not operate in the same way as the old 6th April 1965 base and phrases like the "kink test" entered the tax adviser's vocabulary, as even more complex calculations became necessary. Only the subsequent passage of time has rendered most of these complexities irrelevant in most cases today.

The Conservative Governments of the late 1980s and early 1990s continued to introduce a number of Capital Gains Tax exemptions and reliefs, including some very generous holdover reliefs for reinvestment of gains, as well as substantial increases in the annual exemption.

By the time of the 1997 General Election, the Conservatives were set well on a path towards the abolition of Capital Gains Tax and a return to the pre-1965 situation.

However, as we all know, the Election on 3rd May 1997 brought an historic victory for "New Labour". Those with potential capital gains awaited the seemingly inevitable crackdown.

But when the changes came, they were very far from the draconian measures which some rather hysterical commentators had predicted. In fact, the new Capital Gains Tax regime ushered in by Chancellor Gordon Brown's second Budget on 17th

March 1998 is quite possibly the most generous we have seen since 1965.

Clearly, "New Labour" have recognised that the immense changes in British society over nearly two decades of Conservative Government mean that capital gains are no longer the perquisite of the privileged few, but are now very much a part of life for a significant proportion of the population in the modern economy of investment and enterprise.

The cornerstone of Labour's new Capital Gains Tax regime, Taper Relief, has, from the outset, come in two different tiers, Business Asset Taper Relief and Non-Business Asset Taper Relief.

Since 1998, the rate and availability of Business Asset Taper Relief has been improved significantly, with the maximum relief now reached after just two years, as opposed to the ten year period introduced initially.

Best of all, from 6th April 2004, most commercial (i.e. non-residential) properties are classified as "Business Assets" for Taper Relief purposes.

Non-Business Asset Taper Relief, which is far more relevant to residential property investment, has, however, remained unchanged since its introduction.

4.3 Who Pays Capital Gains Tax?

Capital Gains Tax is payable in the UK by:

i)   Individuals who are UK resident or UK ordinarily resident.
ii)   UK resident trusts.
iii) Non-resident persons trading in the UK through a branch or agency.

In this chapter, we will be concentrating mainly on category (i) above, i.e. UK resident or UK ordinarily resident individuals investing in property.

Individuals who are UK resident or UK ordinarily resident and also UK domiciled are liable for Capital Gains Tax on their worldwide capital gains.

Individuals who are UK resident or UK ordinarily resident but not UK domiciled are always liable for Capital Gains Tax on capital gains arising from the disposal of UK property but only liable for Capital Gains Tax on "foreign" capital gains if and when they remit their disposal proceeds back to the UK.

The tax concepts of residence and domicile are examined in section 3.17 above. Domicile is also covered further in section 5.4 below. Capital Gains Tax also extends to those who are UK ordinarily resident and this will be examined a little further later in section 6.10.

4.4 What is a Capital Gain?

A capital gain is the profit arising on the disposal, in whole or in part, of an asset, or an interest in an asset.

Put simply, the gain is the excess obtained on the sale of the asset over the price paid to buy it. (However, as we will see in the sections that follow, matters rarely remain that simple).

Sometimes, however, assets are held in such a way that their disposal gives rise to an Income Tax charge instead. The same amount of gain cannot be subject to both Income Tax and Capital Gains Tax.

Where both taxes might apply, Income Tax will take precedence, so that no Capital Gains Tax arises. (There is little comfort in this, as the regime of reliefs available under Capital Gains Tax is far more generous than under Income Tax and the latter tax therefore usually produces a higher charge where it applies.)

The most common type of asset sale which gives rise to an Income Tax charge, rather than Capital Gains Tax, is, of course, a sale in the course of a trade. In other words, where the asset is, or is deemed to be, trading stock.

If a man buys sweets to sell in his sweet shop they are quite clearly trading stock and his profits on their sale must be subject to Income Tax and not Capital Gains Tax. This is pretty obvious, because there are usually only two things you can do with sweets, eat them or sell them.

Properties, however, have a number of possible uses. A property purchaser may intend one or more of several objectives:

a) To keep the property for personal use, either as a main residence or otherwise.
b) To provide a home for the use of family or friends.
c) To use the property in a business.
d) To let the property out for profit.
e) To hold the property as an investment.
f) To develop the property for profit.
g) To sell the property on at a profit.

Where objectives (f) and/or (g) are the sole purpose behind the purchase of the property, this will render the ultimate gain on the property's sale a trading profit subject to Income Tax. All of the other objectives make the property a capital investment subject only to Capital Gains Tax.

This is simple enough where the objectives described in (f) and (g) above are either completely absent or the sole purpose of the purchase.

Naturally though, in the majority of cases, objective (g) is present to some degree. This does not necessarily render the gain on the property's sale a trading profit subject to Income Tax. This would only be the case where (g) is the sole or overwhelmingly dominant objective behind the purchase.

In practice, there is often more than one objective present when a property is purchased and objectives (f) and (g) may exist to a lesser or greater extent. In many cases, the correct position is obvious but, in borderline situations, each case has to be decided on its own merits.

Examples:

1. *James bought a house in 1990 which he used as his main residence throughout his ownership. In 1995 he built an extension, which substantially increased the value of the house. He continued to live in the house until eventually selling it in 2004.*

This is clearly a capital gain because James carried on using the house for his personal enjoyment for several years after building the extension. (Furthermore, it will be exempt from Capital Gains Tax, as the house was James' main residence throughout his ownership.)

2. *Charles bought a house in 1990 and used it as his main residence for 5 years. In 1995, he moved into a new house and converted the first one into a number of flats. Following the conversion, Charles let the flats out until he eventually sold the whole property in 2004.*

   Charles' situation is less clear-cut than James. Nevertheless, he has still realised a capital gain as the conversion work was clearly intended as a longer-term investment. (Charles would have a partial exemption under the main residence rules.)

3. *William, a wealthy man with three other properties, bought a derelict barn in 2003. He developed it into a luxury home. Immediately after the development work was complete he put the property on the market and sold it in 2005.*

   This is clearly a trading profit subject to Income Tax. William simply developed the property for profit and never put it to any other use.

4. *Anne bought an old farmhouse in 2002. She lived in the property for 3 months and then moved out while substantial renovation work took place. After the work was completed, she let it out for 6 months. Halfway through the period of the lease she put the property on the market and sold it with completion taking place the day the lease expired.*

   This is what one would call "borderline". Anne has had some personal use of the property, and has let it out, but she has also developed it and sold it after only a short period of ownership. This case would warrant a much closer look at all of the circumstances. It should be decided on the basis of Anne's intentions but who, apart from Anne herself, would ever know what these truly were?

Such a case could go either way. The more Anne can do to demonstrate that her intention had been to hold the property as a long-term investment, the better her chances of success will be. Her personal and financial circumstances will be crucial. For example, if she had got married around the time of the sale, or had got into unexpected financial difficulties, which had forced her to make the sale, then she might successfully argue for Capital Gains Tax treatment.

Note that, just because the profit arising on the sale of an asset is a capital gain, this does not necessarily mean that it is subject to Capital Gains Tax.

A number of assets are exempt from Capital Gains Tax, including:

i) Motor cars (i.e. vehicles of a type commonly used as a private vehicle),

ii) Decorations for valour or gallantry (i.e. medals, etc), where not acquired for money or money's worth,

iii) Government securities, (commonly known as "gilts"),

And, most importantly for property investors:

iv) The taxpayer's only or main residence (see section 4.11 below).

Capital losses derived from exempt assets are also not allowable.

Wealth Warning

Whilst we're on the subject of assets which are exempt for Capital Gains Tax purposes, it might just be worth mentioning something which most people do not appreciate is not exempt: **foreign currency!**

This extends to foreign currency bank accounts (including Euro accounts), although small amounts held purely for personal use (e.g. on holiday) are exempted.

Just thought I ought to mention it.

4.5 The Amount of the Gain

Having established that a gain is subject to Capital Gains Tax, it is next necessary to work out how much the gain is.

As stated in section 4.4 above, the essence of this is that the gain should be the excess obtained on the sale of the asset over the price paid to buy it. This is a reasonable statement of the underlying principle. However, in practice, thanks to the many complexities introduced by tax legislation over nearly 40 years, there are a large number of other factors to be taken into account.

Hence, one has to slightly amend the definition of a capital gain to the following:

"A capital gain is the excess of the actual or deemed proceeds arising on the disposal of an asset over that same asset's base cost."

A shorter version of this is: Gain = Proceeds Less Base Cost

The derivation of "Proceeds" is examined in section 4.6 below and "Base Cost" is covered in sections 4.7 and 4.8.

Note that, for the majority of this Chapter, we will be looking at the rules governing capital gains. Slightly different rules apply to capital losses, which are covered briefly in section 4.24.

There are also cases where, although an asset is held as a capital investment, there is deemed to be no gain and no loss arising on the disposal. The most important instance of this is that of transfers between husband and wife.

4.6 Proceeds

In most cases, the amount of "Proceeds" to be used in the calculation of a capital gain will be the actual sum received on the disposal of the asset. However, from this, the taxpayer may deduct incidental costs in order to arrive at "net proceeds", which is the relevant sum for the purposes of calculating the capital gain.

Example

In July 2004, George sells a house for £375,000. In order to make this sale, he spent £1,500 advertising the property, paid £3,750 in estate agents' fees and paid £800 in legal fees. His net proceeds are therefore £368,950 (£375,000 LESS £1,500, £3,750 and £800).

Remember George – we will be seeing him again!

Now this sounds very simple, but it is not always this easy.

Exceptions

There are a number of cases where the proceeds we must use in the calculation of a capital gain are not simply the actual cash sum received. Three of the most common types of such exceptions are set out below.

Exception 1 – Connected persons

Where the person selling or disposing of the asset is "connected" with the person buying or acquiring it, the open market value of the asset at the time of sale must be used in place of the actual price paid (if any).

Connected persons include:

- Husband or wife (but note that no gain usually arises in such transfers)
- Mother, father or remoter ancestor
- Son, daughter or remoter descendant
- Brother or sister
- Mother-in-law, father-in-law, son-in-law, daughter-in-law, brother-in-law or sister-in-law

- Business partners
- Companies under the control of the other party to the transaction or of any of his/her relatives as above
- Trustees of a trust where the other party to the transaction, or any of his/her relatives as above, is a beneficiary.

Example

Victoria sells a property to her son Edward for £500,000, at a time when its market value is £800,000. She pays legal fees of £475.

Victoria will be deemed to have received net sale proceeds of £800,000 (the market value). The legal fees she has borne are irrelevant, as this was not an "arm's-length" transaction.

Exception 2 – Transactions not at "arms-length"

Where a transaction takes place between "connected persons" as above, there is an automatic assumption that the transaction is not at "arm's-length" and hence market value must always be substituted for the actual proceeds.

There are, however, other instances where the transaction may not be at "arm's-length", such as:

- The transfer of an asset from one partner in an unmarried couple to the other
- A sale of an asset to an employee
- A transaction which is part of a larger transaction
- A transaction which is part of a series of transactions

The effect of these is much the same as before – the asset's market value must be used in place of the actual proceeds, if any.

The key difference from Exception 1 above is that the onus of proof that this is not an "arm's-length" transaction is on the Inland Revenue, rather than there being an automatic assumption that this is the case.

Example

John has a house worth £200,000. If he sold it for this amount, he would have a capital gain of £80,000.

Not wishing to incur a Capital Gains Tax liability, John decides instead to sell the house to his friend Richard for £120,000. However, John only does this on condition that Richard gives him an interest-free loan of £80,000 for an indefinite period.

The condition imposed by John means that this transaction is not at "arm's-length". The correct position is therefore that John should be deemed to have sold the house for £200,000 and still have a capital gain of £80,000.

Exception 3 – Non-cash proceeds

Sometimes all or part of the sale consideration will take a form other than cash.

The sale proceeds to be taken into account in these cases will be the market value of the assets or rights received in exchange for the asset sold.

Example

Matilda is an elderly widow with a large house. She no longer needs such a large house, so she offers it to Stephen, who lives nearby with his wife and young children. Rather than pay the whole amount in cash, Stephen offers £100,000 plus his own much smaller house, which is worth £150,000.

Matilda incurs legal fees of £2,400 on the transaction and also pays Stamp Duty Land Tax of £1,500 to acquire Stephen's house. 75% of the legal fees are for the sale of her old house and the remainder for the purchase of Stephen's house.

Matilda's total sale proceeds are £250,000. This is made up of the cash received plus the market value of the non-cash consideration received, i.e. Stephen's house.

Matilda may deduct her incidental costs of disposal from her proceeds in her Capital Gains Tax calculation. This is unaltered by the existence of non-cash consideration; the transaction has still taken place on "arm's-length" terms.

However, as far as her legal fees are concerned, it is only the element which relates to the disposal of her old house (£1,800) which may be deducted. The element relating to the purchase of Stephen's house will be treated as an acquisition cost of that house, as will the Stamp Duty Land Tax Matilda has paid (see section 5.2 below).

Hence, the net sale proceeds to be used in Matilda's Capital Gains Tax calculation are £248,200 (£250,000 LESS £1,800).

4.7 Base Cost

The "Base Cost" is the amount which may be deducted in the Capital Gains Tax calculation in respect of its cost. The higher the base cost, the less Capital Gains Tax payable!

As before, in most cases, the basic starting point will be the actual amount paid. (But see section 4.8: "Base Cost – Special Situations" below).

To this may be added:

- Incidental costs of acquisition (e.g. legal fees, Stamp Duty Land Tax, etc).
- Enhancement expenditure (e.g. the cost of building an extension to a property).
- Expenditure incurred in establishing, preserving or defending title to, or rights over, the asset (e.g. legal fees incurred as a result of a boundary dispute).

Example

George (remember him from section 4.6?) bought a house in July 1984 for £60,000. He paid Stamp Duty of £600, legal fees of £400 and removal expenses of £800.

Shortly after moving into the house, George spent £3,000 on redecorating it. £1,800 of this related to one of the bedrooms, which was in such a bad state of repair that it was unusable. The remainder of the redecorating expenditure merely covered repainting and wallpapering the other rooms in the house.

In March 1985, George's neighbour erected a new fence a foot inside George's back garden, claiming this was the correct boundary. George had to take legal advice to resolve this problem, which cost him £250, but managed eventually to get the fence moved back to its original position.

In October 1987, the house's roof was badly damaged by hurricane force winds. The repairs cost £20,000, which, unfortunately, George's insurance company refused to pay, claiming he was not covered for an "Act of God".

In May 1995, George did a loft conversion at a cost of £15,000, putting in new windows and creating an extra bedroom. Unfortunately, however, he had not obtained planning permission and, when his neighbour filed a complaint with the council, George was forced to restore the loft to its original condition at a further cost of £8,000.

In August 1998, George had the property extended at a cost of £80,000. He also incurred professional fees of £2,000 obtaining planning permission, etc.

When George eventually sold the property in July 2004 for £375,000, his base cost for the house for Capital Gains Tax purposes was made up as follows:

- Original cost - £60,000.
- Incidental costs of acquisition - £1,000 (legal fees and Stamp Duty, but not the removal expenses, which were a personal cost and not part of the capital cost of the property).
- Enhancement expenditure - £1,800 (restoration of the "unusable" bedroom; the remaining redecoration costs are not allowable, however, as the other rooms were already in a fit state for habitation and George's expenditure was merely due to personal taste, rather than being a capital improvement.).
- Expenditure incurred in defending title to the property - £250 (the legal fees relating to his neighbour's new fence).
- Further enhancement expenditure - £82,000 (the cost of the new extension, including the legal fees incurred to obtain planning permission).

Total base cost: £145,050.

<u>Notes to the example</u>

    i.   If the house were George's only or main residence throughout his ownership, his gain would, in any case, be exempt from Capital Gains Tax. However, we are assuming that this is not the case here for the purposes of illustration.

    ii.   The cost of George's roof repairs do not form part of his base cost. This is not a capital improvement, but rather repairs and maintenance expenditure of a revenue nature.

    iii.   Neither the cost of George's loft conversion, nor the cost of returning the loft to its original condition, form part of his base cost. This is because enhancement or improvement expenditure can only be allowed in the capital gains calculation if the relevant "improvements" are reflected in the state of the property at the time of the sale.

    iv.   Based on net proceeds of £368,950 (see section 4.6), George has a capital gain of £223,900 before indexation (see section 4.9) and other reliefs.

4.8 Base Cost – Special Situations

As before with "Proceeds", there are a number of special situations where base cost is determined by reference to something other than the actual amount paid for the asset.

The major exceptions fall into two main categories:

- The asset was acquired before 31st March 1982 (see 4.8.1 below).
- The asset was not acquired by way of a "bargain at arm's length" (see 4.8.2 to 4.8.6 below).

4.8.1   Assets acquired before 31st March 1982

Due to the "rebasing" of Capital Gains Tax, gains arising due to an asset's increase in value prior to 31st March 1982 are exempt.

Generally speaking, the way that this is achieved is by substituting the asset's market value on 31st March 1982 for its original cost.

Example 4.8 (a)

Alfred bought a house for £20,000 in April 1980. Its market value on 31st March 1982 was £28,000. He sold the house for £200,000 in July 2004.

Alfred should substitute the March 1982 value of £28,000 for his original cost in the calculation of his capital gain.

However, the strict rule is that it is actually the sum which produces the lower gain which should be used. Naturally, whenever there actually is a gain (which will now almost always be the case for a property acquired before March 1982) this means using the higher sum out of March 1982 value and original cost.

Example 4.8 (b)

Ethelred bought a house for £16,500 in June 1981. Its market value on 31st March 1982 was £15,800. He sold the house for £135,000 in July 2004.

In this case, Ethelred should continue to use his original cost of £16,500 in calculating his base cost, as it produces the smaller gain.

Where March 1982 value is being used in the calculation of base cost, the other elements which are normally also included (see section 4.7 above) may still be included provided that they were incurred after 31st March 1982.

Example 4.8 (c)

Canute bought a house for £18,000 in March 1979. He spent £7,000 on an extension in August 1981 and £16,000 on a conservatory in September 1988. He sold the house for £190,000 in December 2004. The house's March 1982 value was £27,500.

Canute's base cost is £43,500, i.e. the March 1982 value PLUS the post-March 1982 enhancement expenditure of £16,000, (but NOT the pre-March 1982 enhancement expenditure of £7,000).

Note that, if the March 1982 value had been less than £23,000, Canute would have reverted to using original *cost, since this would have produced a lower gain. (Because the £7,000 of improvement expenditure incurred in 1981 would then have been included in the base cost).*

Another point, which is worth mentioning here is that, under certain limited circumstances, it is possible to elect that the March 1982 values of assets held by a person at that date should always take precedence over original cost. Most of those who would have benefited from the election will have made it many years ago.

Further rules apply to assets held before 6th April 1965. However, these are seldom needed in practice nowadays.

4.8.2 Inherited assets

Assets are also always "rebased" for Capital Gains Tax purposes on death. Hence, the base cost of any inherited assets is determined by reference to their market value at the date of the previous owner's death.

(Note that, whilst transfers on death are exempt from Capital Gains Tax, they are, of course, subject to Inheritance Tax. See the Taxcafe.co.uk guide *"How To Avoid Inheritance Tax"* for further details.)

Example 4.8 (d)

Albert died on 1st January 1996, leaving his holiday home, a cottage on the Isle of Wight, to his son Edward. The property was valued at £150,000 for probate purposes. In August 2000, Edward has a swimming pool built at the cottage at a cost of £40,000. He then sells the cottage for £287,000 in March 2005.

Edward's base cost is £190,000. His own improvement expenditure (£40,000) is added to the market value of the property when he inherited it. Any expenditure incurred by Albert is, however, completely irrelevant.

4.8.3 Assets acquired from husband or wife

Whenever an asset is transferred between spouses, that transfer is treated as taking place on a no gain/no loss basis.

Furthermore, in the case of a subsequent disposal, the transferee spouse effectively steps into the shoes of the transferor spouse.

Example 4.8 (e)

Henry bought a house for £350,000 in November 1999. He spent £100,000 on capital improvements and then gave the house to his wife Katherine in March 2000. Katherine had the house extended in May 2004 at a cost of £115,000 and then sold it the following February for £750,000.

Katherine's base cost for the house is £565,000. This includes both her own expenditure and her husband's.

This rule applies for the whole of any tax year during any part of which the couple are living together as husband and wife. Separated couples are treated like other "connected persons" (see 4.8.4 below). Divorced couples (following decree absolute) become unconnected persons for tax purposes once more.

The "no gain/no loss" rule does not, however, apply in the case of a transfer on death, when the rules explained at 4.8.2 above take precedence.

4.8.4   Assets acquired from connected persons

As explained in section 4.6 above, the transfer of an asset to a connected person is deemed to take place at market value. Hence, for the person acquiring an asset by way of such a transfer, the market value at that date becomes their base cost.

4.8.5   Other assets acquired by way of a transactions not at "arm's-length"

Again, for the person acquiring the asset, the market value at the date of acquisition becomes their base cost. (See "Exception 2", in section 4.6 above, for further guidance on circumstances where this might arise).

4.8.6   Assets with "held-over gains"

From 6th April 1980 to 13th March 1989, it was possible to elect to hold over the gain arising on the transfer of any asset by way of gift. Since then, it has only been possible to hold over gains arising on transfers by way of gift which are:

- Transfers of business assets, or
- Chargeable transfers for Inheritance Tax purposes.

Furthermore, even in these cases, the ability to hold over a gain was blocked for transfers into a "self-interested trust" on or after 10th December 2003. A "self-interested" trust means a trust which includes the transferor or their spouse as one of its beneficiaries.

The base cost of an asset which was subject to a hold-over election when it was acquired, will be reduced as follows:

- For assets acquired between 1st March 1982 and 5th April 1988: half the amount of the held over gain,
- For other assets acquired with held over gains: the full amount of the held over gain.

Example 4.8 (f)

Arthur owned two properties, "Camelot" and "Elsinore". On 3rd January 1982, he gave Camelot to his son Lancelot. Camelot's market value at that date was £100,000 and Arthur and Lancelot jointly elected to hold over Arthur's gain of £70,000. In 1990 Lancelot had the property extended at a cost of £55,000.

On 12th May 1982, Arthur gave Elsinore to his other son, Merlin. Elsinore's market value at that date was £90,000 and Arthur and Merlin jointly elected to hold over Arthur's gain of £48,000.

Lancelot's base cost for Camelot is £85,000 (£100,000 LESS £70,000 PLUS £55,000 – his own enhancement expenditure is still added on, as normal).

Merlin's base cost for Elsinore is £66,000 (£90,000 LESS HALF OF £48,000).

4.8.7   Assets acquired for non-cash consideration

Where an asset was acquired for non-cash consideration, its base cost will be determined by reference to the market value of the consideration given.

Example 4.8 (g)

> *Julius bought a house in Chester from his friend, Brutus. Instead of paying Brutus in cash, Julius gave him his ancient coin collection, which he had recently had valued at £125,000.*

Julius' base cost in the Chester house will be £125,000.

4.9 Indexation

From March 1982 to April 1998, taxpayers were given a form of relief known as "Indexation Relief", designed to eliminate the purely inflationary element of their capital gains. Indexation relief is still given now to taxpayers disposing of assets held since before April 1998 and hence it remains highly relevant to Capital Gains Tax calculations.

The relief is based on the increase in the retail prices index ("RPI") over the period of the asset's ownership up to April 1998.

Where the base cost of the asset (see sections 4.7 and 4.8 above) is made up of original cost and later enhancement expenditure, each element of the base cost which arose before April 1998 will attract indexation relief at its own appropriate rate.

Example ("George the Third")

In section 4.6, we saw that George received net proceeds of £368,950 for the sale of his house in July 2004. In section 4.7, we saw how his base cost for the house came to £145,050, leaving him with a gain of £223,900.

George is due indexation relief as follows:

i.   From July 1984 to April 1998 on £62,800 (purchase price of £60,000 PLUS acquisition costs of £1,000 PLUS enhancement expenditure of £1,800).

The RPI for July 1984 is 89.1 and the RPI for April 1998 is 162.6. The increase in the RPI over the relevant period is therefore 82.4916%. However, for Capital Gains Tax calculation purposes, the increase in the RPI is always taken to the nearest tenth of a percentage point, i.e. 82.5% in this case.

The indexation relief due on this expenditure is thus £51,810 (82.5% of £62,800).

ii.   From March 1985 to April 1998 on £250 (the legal fees relating to his neighbour's new fence).

The RPI for March 1985 is 92.8, making the increase to April 1998 75.2%. The indexation relief due on this expenditure is thus £188 (75.2% of £250).

George is therefore due indexation relief totalling £51,998, reducing his gain to £171,902 (£223,900 LESS £51,988).

Note to the example

Note that George is not entitled to any indexation relief on his further enhancement expenditure of £82,000 in August 1998. This is because the relief only applies to expenditure before April 1998.

Some terminology

Sometimes, the asset's base cost plus the indexation relief due is known as the "indexed base cost". In George's case this would amount to £197,048.

This can be a slightly misleading concept, however, due to the different treatment of indexation where capital losses arise. (See section 4.24 below).

The remaining gain after indexation (i.e. £171,902 in George's case) is also sometimes known as the "indexed gain".

The maximum relief

The maximum rate of indexation relief applies to assets held throughout the period since the relief's commencement in March 1982. This maximum relief amounts to 104.7%. For example, an asset held on 31st March 1982, which has a base cost of £10,000, would attract indexation relief of £10,470.

A useful list of the applicable indexation relief rates for all disposals by individuals, partnerships or trusts after 5th April 1998 is given in Appendix B at the end of this guide.

Companies

Companies continue to be eligible for indexation relief and hence will attract higher levels of relief than those shown in Appendix B.

4.10 Other Reliefs

It is at this point in the Capital Gains Tax calculation, (i.e. after indexation relief), that other reliefs and exemptions may be claimed, where appropriate. These include:

- The Principal Private Residence ("principal private residence") exemption (for taxpayers selling their current or former only or main residence). This is covered in detail in sections 4.11 to 4.13 below.
- The Private Letting exemption (where a property which is eligible for the principal private residence exemption is or has also been let out as private residential accommodation). Again, this is covered in detail in section 4.11 below.
- Relief for reinvestment of gains in Enterprise Investment Scheme shares or, (until 5th April 2004), Venture Capital Trusts (see section 6.9 below for further details).
- Retirement relief (on business assets, or shares in a personal trading company – this relief ceased to apply for disposals after 5th April 2003).
- Holdover relief on gifts of business assets.

- Holdover relief in respect of chargeable transfers for Inheritance Tax purposes.
- Holdover relief on transfer of a business to a limited company.
- Rollover relief on replacement of business assets.
- Relief for capital losses (see section 4.24 below).

It is important to note that all these reliefs must be claimed BEFORE Taper Relief (see section 4.14 below). In many cases, this effectively devalues these reliefs, especially where the assets concerned are business assets for Taper Relief purposes.

Only the annual exemption (see section 4.19 below) is applied after Taper Relief.

4.11 The Principal Private Residence Exemption

Most people are well aware that the sale of their home is exempt from Capital Gains Tax. In technical terms, this is known as the Principal Private Residence exemption. What is less well known is just how far the principal private residence exemption can extend, especially when combined with other available exemptions and reliefs.

Each unmarried individual, and each legally married couple, is entitled to the principal private residence exemption in respect of their only or main residence. The principal private residence exemption covers the period during which the property was their main residence PLUS, in every case, their last 3 years of ownership.

Example 4.11.1

Elizabeth Windsor bought a flat for £80,000 in January 1995. In January 1999, she married Philip and moved out of her flat. In January 2002, she receives an offer to sell the flat for £120,000, but is concerned about her potential tax liability.

Elizabeth needn't worry. If she makes this sale, her gain on the flat will be exempted under principal private residence. The first 4 years of her ownership are exempt because it was then her main residence and the last 3 years because it was a former main residence.

But what if the property has been let out?

Because the principal private residence exemption always extends to the final three years of ownership of a former main residence, letting the property out for up to three years after you have moved out of it will make no difference to your Capital Gains Tax position if you then go ahead and sell the property. (Income Tax is, of course, due on the rental profits).

If you retain the property for more than three years after it ceased to be your main residence, you will no longer be fully covered by the principal private residence exemption alone. However, at this point, as long as the property is being let out as private residential accommodation, another relief will come into play: Private Letting Relief.

Private Letting Relief is given as the lowest of:

i)   The amount of gain already exempted under principal private residence relief,

ii)   The gain arising as a consequence of the letting period, and

iii)   £40,000.

Usually, it is the lower of (i) and (iii), especially if the property has been let out ever since the owner ceased to reside in it.

Example 4.11.2

Since marrying Philip in January 1999, Elizabeth has been renting her flat out. She turned down the January 2002 offer but in January 2009 she receives an offer of £160,000. Again, she is concerned about her potential tax liability.

Elizabeth still has nothing to worry about. As before, a total of 7 years of her ownership is exempt under principal private residence relief. Her total gain over 14 years is £80,000 (ignoring indexation relief for the time being). 7/14ths (or half) of this is covered by principal private residence relief, leaving £40,000, which is covered by Private Letting Relief.

Hence, Elizabeth still has no Capital Gains Tax liability on her flat!

Note: The general rule here is that a gain of up to £80,000 is covered until at least 2 times (N + 3) years after you first bought the property, (where "N" is the number of years that it was your own main residence, not counting the last three years of ownership).

What if the property was let out <u>before</u> it became your main residence?

Any property which qualifies for partial exemption under principal private residence relief, and which has also been let out as private residential accommodation at <u>any time</u> during the taxpayer's ownership, is also eligible for Private Letting Relief.

Hence, although in our example we have been looking at a <u>former</u> main residence, which is subsequently let out, Private Letting Relief will apply equally in a case where a property is let out first and then subsequently becomes the owner's main residence.

If, in Example 4.11.2, Elizabeth had instead rented her flat out from 1995 to 1997, then lived in it as her main residence for four years before continuing to rent it out again, the result would have been exactly the same.

(Note that Elizabeth's flat would have had to be Philip's main residence too after they got married, as a married couple is only allowed one main residence for principal private residence relief purposes.)

One thing to watch with this approach though, is that there is no additional benefit to be derived from the extension to the principal private residence exemption for a former main residence's last three years of ownership if, in fact, it is still your main residence throughout that time in any case.

The Impact of other reliefs

Three other reliefs will have a major impact where part of a gain is already exempted under principal private residence relief:

i)   Indexation relief (see section 4.9 above).
ii)   Taper relief (see section 4.14 below).
iii)   The annual exemption (see section 4.19 below), which stands at £8,200 for the tax year ending on 5th April 2005.

Example 4.11.3

Elizabeth turns down the January 2009 offer and continues to rent the flat out. In January 2012 she receives an offer of £180,000. Once more, she is concerned about her potential tax liability.

This time it is necessary to carry out a full calculation of Elizabeth's capital gain.

Her total gain before indexation is £100,000. She is, however, entitled to indexation relief of £9,120, producing an indexed gain of £90,880.

As before, 7 years of her ownership is exempt under principal private residence relief. This now represents 7/17ths of her total period of ownership, so £37,422 of her indexed gain is exempt, leaving £53,458 chargeable. Of this, a further £37,422 is exempted by Private Letting Relief, leaving only £16,036.

Having owned the property for more than 10 years, Elizabeth gets taper relief of 40%, leaving a tapered gain of £9,621, which, by 2012, is very likely to be covered by her annual exemption (£8,200 indexed up for eight years), leaving her with no Capital Gains Tax to pay!

Notes to Example 4.11.3

i)   If you are checking these calculations, you may notice that the principal private residence exemption actually works out at £37,421.18. This brings out a very minor, but nevertheless beneficial, principle – i.e.: you are always allowed to **round up** reliefs and exemptions to the nearest £1.

ii)   Private Letting Relief has been restricted to the lowest of the three items detailed above. In this case, this is the amount already exempted under principal private residence relief.

Principal Private Residence Summary

In our quite realistic example, Elizabeth has managed to make a tax-free capital gain of £100,000 despite living in her flat for only 4 years out of a total of 17. This remarkable result arises due to the impact of a number of reliefs which each build onto the basic exemption already available for a former main residence.

These reliefs are invaluable to both those with a former home they now wish to sell and those who wish to plan for future tax-free capital growth.

Planning Ahead

One can readily see how the principal private residence exemption and its associated reliefs could be used to allow a taxpayer to invest in property free from Capital Gains Tax. This subject is covered in greater depth in Chapter Six later in the guide.

4.12 Extending the Principal Private Residence Exemption

There are a number of special cases where the principal private residence exemption may extend even further. A brief summary follows.

4.12.1 Gardens and Grounds

There have been a large number of cases before the Courts over the question of whether the "grounds" of a house, including some of the subsidiary outbuildings, are covered by the principal private residence exemption.

In the usual situation, where a house has a reasonably normal sized garden and perhaps a shed, a garage or other small outbuildings, there is no doubt that the entire property is covered by the principal private residence exemption.

Naturally, we are talking here only of the situation where there is no use of any of the property other than private residential occupation.

Where the whole property is let out at some point, so that private letting relief applies, the garden and "modest" grounds continue to be covered by the relevant reliefs in the same way as already outlined in section 4.11 above.

The general rule of thumb for grounds is that the Revenue will accept them as being a normal part of the property where they do not exceed half a hectare (1.235 acres) in area. Beyond this, it is necessary to argue that the additional space is required "for the reasonable enjoyment of the dwelling-house as a residence".

What does this mean? Well, unfortunately, this is one of those rather enigmatic answers which Judges love to give and which can only be decided on an individual case-by-case basis.

The whole situation changes once any part of the property is used for any other purpose. Here the position differs for buildings or gardens and grounds.

For gardens and grounds, they will obtain the same exemptions that are due on the house itself as long as they are part of the "private residence" at the time of sale.

For subsidiary buildings, it becomes necessary to apportion any gain arising between the periods of residential occupation and the periods of non-residential use.

Example 4.12.1.1

Lady Jane has a large house with grounds having a total area of half a hectare. Her property lies next to a major amusement park and, for several years, she leased half her grounds to the park for use as a car park.

Within the half of her grounds let to the amusement park there is a small outbuilding. Whilst she was letting the space to the amusement park, this outbuilding was used as the parking attendant's hut.

In 1999, the amusement park gave up its lease over Lady Jane's grounds and she hired a landscape gardener to restore them.

The outbuilding reverted to its previous use as a storage shed for garden equipment.

In 2005, Lady Jane sold the entire property. Apart from the lease of the car park, the whole property had been used as her main residence throughout her ownership.

Lady Jane's main house and her entire grounds will be fully covered by the principal private residence exemption. However, the element of her gain relating to the outbuilding must be apportioned between the periods of private use and the period of non-residential use. The non-residential element of the gain will be chargeable to Capital Gains Tax.

> **Tax Tip**
> Lady Jane may have been better off if she had demolished the outbuilding prior to the sale of her house. No part of her gain would then have related to this building and her entire gain would have been covered by the principal private residence exemption. Naturally, it is only worth doing this if demolishing the building does not impact on the whole property's sale price by more than the amount of the potential tax saving.

4.12.2 "Doing The Place Up"

Many people buy a "run-down" property and then embark on substantial renovation works before occupying it as their own main residence.

The tax rules cater for this situation and the principal private residence exemption specifically extends to cover any period of up to one year during which the taxpayer is unable to occupy a newly acquired house due to either:

i)   An unavoidable delay in selling their old property, or
ii)   The need to await the finalisation of renovation or construction work on the new property.

During this period, it is possible for both the old and new properties to simultaneously be covered by the principal private residence exemption. Of course, the scope for claiming this exemption is lost if the new property is being used for some other purpose between purchase and initial occupation as the taxpayer's main residence. (Although the private letting exemption could apply to this period in appropriate circumstances.)

Under exceptional circumstances, the Revenue may allow this initial period to be extended to up to two years. However, if the delay extends beyond the first year or beyond any additional period which the Revenue permit, then the principal private residence exemption is lost for the whole of the period prior to occupation of the property.

4.12.3 Temporary Absences

The principal private residence exemption will remain available in full for certain temporary periods of absence, as follows:

i)   Any single period of up to three years or shorter periods totalling no more than three years, regardless of the reason,

ii)   A period of up to four years when the taxpayer, or their spouse, is required to work elsewhere by reason of their employment or their place of work, and

iii)   A period of any length when the taxpayer or their spouse is working in an office or employment whose duties are all performed outside the UK.

These temporary absences are only covered by the principal private residence exemption if:

a) The taxpayer occupies the property as their main residence for both a period before the absence period <u>and</u> a period following the absence period, and

b) Neither the taxpayer nor their spouse have any interest in any other property capable of being treated as their main residence under the principal private residence exemption.

In the case of absences under (ii) or (iii) above, the Revenue may, by concession, sometimes accept that the taxpayer was unable to resume occupation of the property following their absence if they are then required to work elsewhere on their return.

4.12.4 Job-Related Accommodation

In many occupations, it is necessary, or desirable, for the taxpayer to live in accommodation specifically provided for the purpose. Examples include:

- Caretakers
- Police officers
- Pub landlords
- Members of the armed services
- Teachers at boarding schools
- The Prime Minister and the Chancellor of the Exchequer

For people in this type of situation, the principal private residence exemption may be extended to a property which they own and which they eventually intend to adopt as their main residence. In these circumstances, the principal private residence exemption will thus cover the period during which the taxpayer is living in "job-related" accommodation, despite the fact that their own property is not their main residence at that time.

4.12.5 Dependant Relatives

A property occupied before 6th April 1988 by a "dependant relative" may be covered by the principal private residence exemption. This is a rare exception to the general rule that each individual taxpayer or married couple may only have one property exempted as their main residence at any given time.

For this purpose, a "dependant relative" must be either
 a) The taxpayer's mother or mother-in-law, or
 b) Another relative who is either elderly or dependent on them by reason of ill-health or disability.

(Rather insultingly, the Revenue class anyone over the male state retirement age of 65 as "elderly"!)

4.12.6 Properties Held in Trust

A trust is a separate legal entity in its own right for tax purposes and here the principal private residence exemption is no exception. The exemption extends to a property held by a trust when the property is the only or main residence of one or more of the trust's beneficiaries.

However, from 10th December 2003, the principal private residence exemption is not available on a property held by a trust if a hold-over relief claim was made on the transfer of that property into the trust.

In some cases this may lead to a difficult decision:

- Decline to make a hold-over relief claim at the outset and pay some Capital Gains Tax immediately, or

- Make the hold-over relief claim and risk paying a great deal more Capital Gains Tax on the eventual sale of the property.

4.12.7 Second Homes

As already stated, each unmarried individual and each legally married couple can (generally) only have one main residence covered by the principal private residence exemption at any given time. Many people, however, have more than one private residence.

When someone acquires a second (or subsequent) private residence they may, at any time within two years of the date that the new property first becomes available to them as a residence, elect which of their properties is to be regarded as their main residence for the purpose of the principal private residence exemption.

The election must be made in writing, addressed to "Her Majesty's Inspector of Taxes" and sent to the taxpayer's tax office (see section 1.6). An unmarried individual must sign the election personally in order for it to be effective. A married couple must both sign the election.

There is no particular prescribed form for the election, although the following example wording would be suitable for inclusion:

> "In accordance with section 222(5) Taxation of Chargeable Gains Act 1992, [I/We] hereby nominate [Property] as [my/our] main residence with effect from [Date*]."

* - The first such election which an individual or a married couple makes in respect of any new combination of residences will automatically be treated as coming into effect from the beginning of the period to which it relates – i.e. from the date on which they first held that new combination of residences. It is this first election for the new combination of residences to which the two year time limit applies.

However, once an election is in place, it may subsequently be changed, by a further written notice given to the Inspector under the same procedure, at any time. Such a new election may be given retrospective effect, if desired, by up to two years. We will look at the possible benefits of this further in Chapter Six.

Example 4.12.7.1

Alfred lives in a small flat in Southampton where he works. In September 2003, he also buys a house on the Isle of Wight and starts spending his weekends there. In August 2005, Alfred realises that his Isle of Wight house has appreciated in value significantly since he bought it. His small mainland flat has not increased in value quite so significantly. He therefore elects, before the expiry of the two year time limit, that his island house is his main residence.

In 2007 Alfred sells the Isle of Wight house at a substantial gain, which is fully exempted by the principal private residence exemption.

Note in this example that Alfred's flat will not be counted as his main residence from September 2003 until the time of sale of his island house. However, should he sell the flat, his final three years of ownership will be covered by the principal private residence exemption.

Tax Tip
As soon as Alfred decided to sell his Isle of Wight house, he should have submitted a new main residence election nominating the Southampton flat as his main residence once more, with effect from a date two years previously. This would give an extra two years of principal private residence exemption on the flat, whilst leaving the Isle of Wight house fully exempt as long as he sold it within one year after making the new election (i.e. within three years after the date that it was now deemed to cease to be his main residence).

Regardless of any election, however, a property may only be a main residence for principal private residence purposes if it is, in fact, the taxpayer's own private residence. Hence, a property being let out cannot be covered by the principal private residence exemption whilst it is being let. (It could nevertheless still attract the private letting exemption if it were the taxpayer's main residence at some other time).

In the absence of any election, the question of which property is the taxpayer's main residence has to be determined on the facts of the case. Often the answer to this will be obvious but, in borderline cases, the Revenue may determine the position to the taxpayer's detriment. Clearly then, it is <u>always</u> wise to make the election!

Note that the principal private residence exemption applies in exactly the same way to any property held overseas, where the circumstances dictate. The exemption applies to the taxpayer's main residence, not, as some people have mistakenly thought (to their cost) their main <u>UK</u> residence.

4.13 Putting a Part of Your Home to Other Uses

Whenever any part of your home is put to some use other than your own private residential occupation, you are inevitably putting your principal private residence exemption at risk. In this section, we will look at some of the most common situations and their tax implications.

4.13.1 Taking A Lodger

The Revenue generally accept that taking in one individual lodger does not necessitate any restriction to the principal private residence exemption. In this context, a "lodger" is someone who, whilst having their own bedroom, will otherwise live as a member of the taxpayer's household.

As a general rule, where "rent-a-room" relief is available for Income Tax purposes (or would be if the level of rent were lower – see section 3.12), then the principal private residence exemption is likely to be unaffected.

4.13.2 Other lettings – within the same "dwelling"

Where a part of the house is let out under other circumstances, the principal private residence exemption will be restricted. However, Private Letting Relief (see section 4.11 above) is available to cover this restriction in very much the same way as it applies to the letting out of the whole property.

Example 4.13.2.1

Robert bought his five-storey house for £200,000 in 1989. From 1997 to 2003 he let the top two floors out as a flat. He then resumed occupation of the whole house, before selling it in 2005 for £650,000.

Robert's total gain is £450,000 (we are ignoring indexation relief in this example, although, in reality, it would apply). This gain is covered by the principal private residence exemption as follows:

Lower three floors – The gain of £270,000 (three fifths of the total) is fully covered by the principal private residence exemption.
Upper two floors – The gain of £180,000 is covered by the principal private residence exemption from 1989 to 1997 AND for the last three years of Robert's ownership, a total of 11 years out of 16. Hence, £123,750 of this gain is exempt, leaving £56,250 chargeable.

Robert can then claim Private Letting Relief of the lowest of:

i) The amount of principal private residence exemption on the <u>whole</u> property -£393,750 (i.e. £270,000 PLUS £123,750),
ii) The gain arising by reason of the letting (£56,250), or
iii) £40,000.

The relief is thus £40,000, leaving Robert with a gain of only £16,250 before taper relief and the annual exemption (hence, chances are that he has only a negligible Capital Gains Tax liability – even despite us ignoring indexation relief!).

Now, all that Robert probably did was to fit a few locks to a few doors in order to separate the flat from his own home. As a result, re-occupying the whole property was a simple matter and when he came to sell it, it remained a single "dwelling" for tax purposes. The situation would have been quite different if he had carried out extensive conversion work in order to create a number of separate dwellings.

4.13.3 Conversions

Where a property has undergone extensive conversion work, it no longer remains a single dwelling for tax purposes. This is what the Inland Revenue refer to as a "Change of Use" and it has a wider-ranging impact than merely letting out part of your home.

Example 4.13.3.1

David bought a large detached house for £160,000 in 1993. He lived in the whole house for one year and then converted it into two separate, semi-detached, houses. He continued to live in one of these, but rented the other one out. The conversion work cost £40,000, bringing his total costs up to £200,000.

In 2005, David sold both houses for £300,000 each, making a total gain of £400,000 (again, we are ignoring indexation relief in order to simplify the example).

David's gain will be treated as arising equally on each house. The £200,000 gain on the house which he retained as his own home will be fully covered by the principal private residence exemption.

However, David's £200,000 gain on the other house will only be covered by the principal private residence exemption for one year out of his twelve years of ownership. His principal private residence exemption on this house thus amounts to only £16,667, leaving a taxable gain of £183,333 (before taper relief and annual exemption and ignoring indexation relief).

Note the two very important differences here to the previous example, both of which occur because the rented house was no longer a part of the same dwelling, namely:

i) The principal private residence exemption is not available for the last three years of ownership.
ii) No private letting relief is available.

Tax Tip

David would have improved his position dramatically if he had spent some time living in the other semi-detached property after the conversion.

4.13.4 Using Part Of Your Home Exclusively For Business Purposes

Where any part of the property is used exclusively for business purposes, the principal private residence exemption is not available for that part of the property for the relevant period.

The effect on the principal private residence exemption is the same whether part of the property is being used exclusively in the taxpayer's own business or is being rented out for use in someone else's. However, where it is the taxpayer's own business which is concerned, then this part of the property becomes "business property" for the purposes of a number of tax reliefs, including rollover relief and holdover relief for gifts.

The "business" part of the property may also become a "business asset" for taper relief purposes (see section 4.16).
(Property rented out for use in someone else's business will, in most cases, be treated as "business property" for Taper Relief purposes from 6th April 2004. Property rented to an unquoted trading company has been eligible for Business Asset Taper relief since 6th April 2000.)

As in section 4.13.3 above, where the principal private residence exemption is restricted under these circumstances, there is no additional relief for the last three years of ownership and, of course, no private letting relief.

4.13.5 Non-Exclusive Business Use ("The Home Office")

Where part of the home is used non-exclusively for business purposes, there is no restriction on the principal private residence exemption. This is a fairly common situation amongst professionals who work from an office or study within their home. To safeguard the principal private residence exemption in such situations, it is wise to restrict the taxpayer's Income Tax claim in respect of the office's running costs (as a proportion of household expenses) to, say, 95%, in order to reflect the room's occasional private use.

Hence, if the office is one of four rooms in the house (excluding hallways, kitchen, bathrooms and lavatories), one would claim 95% of one quarter of the household running costs.

For this purpose, just about any kind of private use will suffice, such as:

- A guest bedroom.
- Additional storage space for personal belongings.
- A music room.
- A library.

Naturally, it makes sense to adopt some form of private use which will only lead to a small reduction in the Income Tax claim.

> **Tax Tip**
> An expense deduction for Income Tax purposes (see section 3.7) may be claimed by property investors who use part of their own home as an office from which to run their business.

4.13.6 No Use At All

The principal private residence exemption is not restricted merely because part of the house is not used. This contrasts, however, with the situation for outbuildings or gardens and grounds (see section 4.12.1), where actual use for private residential purposes is required.

4.14 Taper Relief – Introduction

Taper relief was introduced by Chancellor Gordon Brown's second Budget on 17th March 1998 and applies to all asset disposals after 5th April 1998. The new relief was designed to replace two existing reliefs:

- Indexation relief (which, for individuals, partnerships and trusts, ceased to accumulate any further after April 1998 – see section 4.9 above).

- Retirement relief (which was gradually phased out and finally abolished altogether on 6th April 2003).

Taper relief applies at two rates, as follows:

- Business Asset Taper Relief, and
- Non-Business Asset Taper Relief.

In either case, the relief is given as a percentage of the gain remaining after all other reliefs, except for the annual exemption (section 4.19), have been claimed.

Example

> John has a gain of £30,000 after indexation and any other relevant reliefs, but before Taper Relief. He is eligible for Taper Relief at 10%. His gain after Taper Relief, or "Tapered Gain", is therefore £27,000.

Quick Overview

Business asset taper relief will exempt 75% of your gain after only two years of ownership.

Non-business asset taper relief takes three years to give you anything at all (5%) and takes ten years to rise to a maximum of 40%.

The difference, as you can see, in both time and the rate of relief, is enormous!

4.15 Non-Business Asset Taper Relief

On the disposal of any asset which does not qualify as a "business asset" (section 4.16), the taxpayer is entitled to Taper Relief at the lower, or "non-business" rate.

Hence, this lower rate will generally apply to most <u>residential</u> property investments.

One major exception to this is any property used in a business which qualifies as the commercial letting of "furnished holiday accommodation" (see section 3.11).

Whilst this is not quite deemed to be a "trade" for tax purposes, it nevertheless attracts many trading-related reliefs and such properties will be treated as business assets for Taper Relief purposes.

Prior to 6th April 2004, the lower taper rate generally also applied to most other investment property. However, from that date, most non-residential property qualifies as a "business asset".

This will benefit commercial property investors greatly. The new, wider, definition of business property is examined further in section 4.16 below.

The Non-Business Asset Taper Relief rate will also apply to a proportion of the gain where:

- The asset is used only partly for a qualifying business purpose, or

- The asset only qualified as a business asset during part of the period of ownership after 5th April 1998.

The second point above will now arise in a great many situations and we will be looking further at the implications of this in section 4.18.

The Rate of Non-Business Asset Taper Relief

The rates of relief have remained the same since its introduction on 6th April 1998, and are as follows:

- For assets held less than three years: Nil
- For assets held for three years but less than four: 5%
- For assets held for four years but less than five: 10%
- For assets held for five years but less than six: 15%
- For assets held for six years but less than seven: 20%
- For assets held for seven years but less than eight: 25%
- For assets held for eight years but less than nine: 30%
- For assets held for nine years but less than ten: 35%
- For assets held for ten years or more: 40%

Assets held before 6th April 1998

The rates set out above have to be adapted in the case of assets already held when Taper Relief was first introduced on 6th April 1998. Two adjustments are required:

- Firstly, in applying the ownership periods set out above, any period of ownership prior to 6th April 1998 is disregarded, but

- To compensate for this, an additional year is counted in respect of any assets held before 17th March 1998.

Example ("George the Fourth")

You may remember from section 4.9 above that, after indexation relief, George had a gain of £171,902 on the sale of his house in July 2004. We now refer to this as the "untapered gain".

George has owned the house since July 1984. His total period of ownership is therefore 20 years. However, for Taper Relief purposes, George can only count the period since 6th April 1998. This gives him six years of ownership for Taper Relief purposes.

But, as he owned the property before 17th March 1998, George gets an additional "bonus" year, meaning that he is deemed to have owned the property for seven years for Taper Relief purposes.

Therefore, George gets Taper Relief at 25%. This amounts to £42,976, leaving him with a tapered gain of £128,926.

Note that the same rate of Taper Relief applies to the whole of George's gain. It makes no difference that some of his enhancement expenditure was incurred after 17th March 1998, all that matters is the date that he originally purchased the property.

It would have been different if George had made a completely new purchase, e.g. an adjacent strip of land. In that case, the Taper Relief would have to be worked out separately for the new asset. However, this does not apply here, as George had merely enhanced an existing asset.

4.16 Business Asset Taper Relief Principles

As the name suggests, Business Asset Taper Relief applies to business assets.

Gordon Brown has had some difficulty in defining what he considers to be a "business asset". He started out with one set of rules in 1998, expanded them quite significantly in April 2000, tinkered a little more in 2001 (which he back-dated to April 2000) and changed them yet again with effect from 6th April 2004.

The latest changes are the most significant and most beneficial for property investors and mean that, from 6th April 2004, most non-residential property is likely to qualify as a "business asset".

Wealth Warning

Where an asset which only qualifies as a business asset with effect from 6th April 2004 was also held before that date, it will only be partly eligible for business asset taper relief.

We will look at the impact of this in more detail in section 4.18.

With effect from 6th April 2004, any asset (including property) will be regarded as a business asset where it is used for the purposes of a trade carried on by:

a) A sole trader,
b) A partnership,
c) A trust,
d) The estate of a deceased person, or
e) A qualifying company (see below).

(Partnerships only qualify here as long as at least one member of the partnership falls under one of the other headings above.) The trading entity does not need to be in any way connected with the owner of the asset. A company will be a "qualifying company" for this purpose under any of the following circumstances:

i)   Whenever the company is an **unquoted trading company**. (Broadly, this means that, in addition to qualifying as a trading company, the company must also not be listed on any recognised stock exchange.)

ii) When the company is a **quoted trading company and the individual** claiming the taper relief (i.e. the property owner) **is an** officer or **employee** of that company or of another company that is a member of the same group of companies or which may reasonably be considered to be part of the same commercial association of companies.

iii) When the company is a **quoted trading company and the individual** claiming the taper relief **owns** enough shares to enable **at least 5%** of the voting rights in the company to be exercised.

iv) When **the individual** claiming the taper relief is an officer or **employee** of the company, or of another company as in (ii) above, and **does not have a 'material interest'** in the company.

     Broadly speaking, this means that the individual concerned, together with any 'connected persons' (see Appendix B) does not hold, and cannot control, more than 10% of any class of shares in the company.

Note that the qualifying company definition given here is also used to determine whether any shares or securities which an individual holds in that company qualify as business assets.

Summary: Position from 6th April 2004

In summary, almost any property you own which you either use yourself in a trading activity, or which you rent out and which your tenants use in a trade, will qualify as a business asset from 6th April 2004. The major exception arises where the tenant is a quoted company, unless you can fall under (ii), (iii) or (iv) above.

Tax Tip

If you are letting a property to a quoted company, you will not generally qualify for business asset taper relief.

However, if you were an employee of that company, you would be entitled to business asset taper relief.

To be an "employee" for this purpose, you could take on any job you like, and part-time work qualifies.

Don't think it's worth it? Take a look as the example below.

Example

Harry Grout is a commercial property investor. In May 2004, he buys a large retail property and lets it out to Sainways plc, a major supermarket chain.

In June 2007, Harry sells the property, realising a £1,000,000 capital gain. He is entitled to non-business asset taper relief of only 5%, leaving a tapered gain of £950,000 and giving Harry a Capital Gains Tax bill of £380,000.

John Barraclough is another commercial property investor who buys a large retail property in May 2004. John lets his property out to Tesda plc, another major supermarket chain. At the same time, he also takes a job with Tesda plc, 3 hours a week on a Saturday afternoon as a "greeter". (One of those people who *says "hello, welcome to Tesda" just as you've walked in the door. I'm not sure of the point of these, but we'll soon see the point for John.)*

John also sells his property at a gain of £1,000,000 in June 2007. He is entitled to business asset taper relief of 75%, leaving a tapered gain of only £250,000 and a Capital Gains Tax bill of just £100,000.

John probably didn't earn much as a "greeter", but he saved £280,000 in Capital Gains Tax!

Note that John only needed to hold the property for two years to get his maximum taper relief. (In the case of a sale after only two years, he would have saved £300,000.) However, he needed to keep his job for as long as he held the property, or else he would have lost some of his taper relief.

Assets held before 6th April 2004

Before 6th April 2004, the definition of "business assets" (other than shares and securities), for taper relief purposes, was broadly as follows:

i)   Any asset used for the purposes of a trade carried on by the individual who owns it, or a partnership of which he or she is a member,

ii)   Any asset used for the purposes of a trade carried on by a qualifying company (or group of companies), or

iii) Any asset used for the purposes of an office or employment held by the individual owning the asset whose employer carries on a trade.

The definition of a "qualifying company" was the same during the period from 6th April 2000 to 5th April 2004 as set out under the new rules applying from 6th April 2004 onwards above.

Prior to 6th April 2000, the "qualifying company" rules were much more difficult to satisfy. This will continue to be relevant to anyone disposing of a property which they held before that date and were letting to a company at that time.

The Relevance of Trading

As can be seen, the definition of "business asset" is highly dependent on the question of what exactly constitutes a "trade" or a "trading company". This is a new and rapidly developing area of tax law.

As far as companies are concerned, the general requirement is that at least 80% of the company's activities must constitute trading.

Sadly, the commercial letting of property is not considered to be a "trade" for tax purposes.

This means that a company which lets out commercial property would not be a qualifying company for taper relief purposes, despite the fact that most such lettings, when made by an individual property owner, would now attract taper relief.

Unfortunately, the definition of a "trade" for taper relief purposes is rather circular:

> "A 'trade' means a trade, profession or vocation conducted on a commercial basis with a view to realisation of profits."

Apart from telling us that we can include professions (e.g. accountants) and vocations (e.g. doctors) and that we must be at least attempting to make a profit, this definition rather unhelpfully falls back on stating that a "trade is a trade"!

This, as explained in chapter two, is where the Inland Revenue will tend to fall back on trying to have their cake and eat it – deciding whether you have a trade when it suits them!

Most cases are obvious, of course, such as the proverbial sweet shop. In more doubtful cases, it is best to take professional advice.

Lastly, as mentioned earlier in section 4.15, remember that furnished holiday lettings will qualify as business assets for taper relief purposes.

Property Investments as Business Assets

At this point, it is worth revisiting the possible uses for property which were previously examined in section 4.4 above. These were:

a)   To keep the property for personal use, either as a main residence or otherwise.
b)   To provide a home for the use of family or friends.
c)   To use the property in a business.
d)   To let the property out for profit.
e)   To hold the property as an investment.
f)   To develop the property for profit.
g)   To sell the property on at a profit.

- Properties falling under (a) or (b) can never qualify as business assets for Taper Relief purposes (except under the circumstances outlined in section 4.13.4 above, and even then only if the business activity qualifies as a "trade").

- Properties falling under (c) will qualify as business assets, as long as the "business" concerned qualifies as a "trade" for tax purposes. Unfortunately, however, an office used to run a property investment business would not itself qualify.

- Properties falling under (d) will now qualify as business assets if they are let to qualifying businesses (as explained above) for use in their trade. Other than the notable exception for furnished holiday accommodation, residential property is, however, unlikely to qualify.

- For properties falling under (e), the position depends on what use they are put to in the meantime and, for the reasons explained in section 4.4, the whole question is irrelevant to properties falling wholly under (f) or (g).

4.17 The Rate of Business Asset Taper Relief

Gordon Brown has also had some difficulty in settling on a set of rates for business asset taper relief. Initially, in 1998, the rates introduced would have taken 10 years to reach their full impact.

(As this coincided with the phased withdrawal of retirement relief, this caused quite a lot of anguish amongst small and medium-sized businesses at the time.)

He improved the business asset taper rates significantly in 2000, reducing the minimum qualifying period to only four years. However, before anyone had even had a chance to clock up four years under the taper relief regime, he had changed them again, to the two year minimum period which we have today.

Thankfully, for those of us who are getting truly exasperated at having to explain the Chancellor's continually changing moods on this subject, he stated in his latest Budget speech on 17th March 2004, that he is now "satisfied with the Capital Gains Tax regime". Phew!

The Current Rates

For disposals made any time after 5th April 2002 the rates of business asset taper relief are:

- Assets held less than one year: Nil
- Assets held for one year, but less than two years: 50%
- Assets held for two years or more: 75%

Previously, for disposals made between 6th April 2000 and 5th April 2002, the rates were:

- Assets held less than one year: Nil
- Assets held for one year, but less than two years: 12.5%
- Assets held for two years after 5th April 1998, but less than three: 25%
- Assets held for three years or more after 5th April 1998: 50%
- (There was another rate for assets held for four years or more, but the system was changed before it ever became relevant.)

Unlike the lower, Non-Business rate, there is no "bonus year" for Business Asset Taper Relief.

4.18 "Hybrid" Taper Relief

Where any asset has been a business asset for only part of the period of ownership since 6th April 1998, whether because of changes in the "business asset" definition, or because of actual changes in use, it will attract a type of "hybrid" Taper Relief. This involves getting the Business Asset Taper Relief rate on a proportion of the gain and the non-business asset rate on the remainder.

Assets which are in this situation, and thus subject to a restriction in the amount of taper relief available, are sometimes referred to as having "tainted taper".

An asset subject to tainted taper will not be eligible for the full rate of taper relief until it has qualified as a business asset for a full **10 years!**

Hence, any property held before 6th April 2004, which only starts to qualify as a business asset from that date onwards, will not be eligible for the full maximum rate of taper relief (75%) until 6th April 2014.

To demonstrate the impact of "tainted taper" in practice, let's look at an example:

Example

Reggie owns a retail unit which he rents out to an unconnected partnership business, "Perrin & Co.". Although Reggie has owned the property since January 1996, it only starts to qualify as a business asset from 6th April 2004.

On 6th April 2006, Reggie sells the property, realising a capital gain, after indexation relief, of £100,000.

As the taper regime started on 6th April 1998, Reggie is deemed to have held the property for eight years for taper relief purposes.

Of these eight years, the property only qualified as a business asset for two. Hence, 2/8ths of Reggie's gain qualifies for business asset taper relief at 75%.

The remaining 6/8ths of Reggie's gain is only eligible for non-business asset taper relief. The bonus year (see section 4.15) applies for this purpose, giving Reggie an effective nine years of non-business asset taper, or 35%.

Reggie's taper relief is thus calculated as follows:

Business asset taper relief:
£100,000 x 2/8 x 75% =   £18,750

Non-Business asset taper relief:
£100,000 x 6/8 x 35% =   £26,250

Total: £45,000

As we can see, in this example, the property owner ends up with an effective "hybrid" taper relief rate of 45%. This rate will slowly improve, day by day, until reaching the full maximum rate of 75% on 6th April 2014.

Incidentally, it is also worth noting that Reggie starts to get **some** business asset taper relief immediately on 6th April 2004. It is not necessary for the property to have been a business asset for a year before he gets **any** business asset taper relief at all, it is only necessary that he has held the property for at least one year.

Partial "Non-Business" Use

A similar situation arises where a part of the property is used for a non-qualifying purpose. Let's look at another example to illustrate this.

Example

Arkwright purchases an office building called "Granville House" on 6th April 2004. Granville House is sub-divided into six office units, all of equal size.

Four of these units are let to qualifying businesses for taper relief purposes, but the other two are let to quoted companies which do not qualify for taper relief purposes as far as Arkwright is concerned (i.e. he is not an employee of either of these *companies and nor does he own 5% of the shares in either of them).*

Two years later, Arkwright sells Granville House at a considerable gain.

4/6ths of Arkwright's gain on Granville House will qualify for business asset taper relief of 75%.

The remaining 2/6ths will not qualify for any taper relief. (Non-business asset taper relief does not apply until an asset has been held for at least three years.)

Combating Tainted Taper

Tainted taper lasts for up to ten years. It will therefore often be worth considering taking steps to combat it.

A transfer of property with tainted taper into a discretionary trust will re-start the taper relief clock and will often allow maximum taper relief to be obtained in two years instead of ten.

Unfortunately, however, from 10th December 2003, any transfers into a "self-interested trust" may potentially give rise to an immediate Capital Gains Tax liability. This applies whenever the transferor or their spouse is able to benefit from the transferee trust.

Such transfers are, however, still worth considering under the following circumstances:

- Where the transferee trust has different beneficiaries (e.g. children of the transferor).

- Where a disposal of the property would not currently give rise to any significant Capital Gains Tax liability (e.g. transferring your own former main residence prior to converting it into office premises).

- Where the Capital Gains Tax liability arising now is far outweighed by the likely future savings (although this does, of course, carry a major element of risk).

4.19 The Annual Exemption

Each individual taxpayer is entitled to an annual exemption for every tax year.

The annual exemption is available to exempt from Capital Gains Tax an amount of capital gains after all other reliefs have been claimed, including the compulsory set-off of capital losses arising in the same tax year. Where capital losses are brought forward from previous tax years, however, the set-off is limited in such a way as to enable the taxpayer to make use of their annual exemption.

Any unused annual exemption is simply lost. It cannot be carried forward. Although it cannot be guaranteed, the exemption generally rises each year in line with inflation.

The amount of the annual exemption available to individual taxpayers for the last few years is:

2000/2001: £7,200
2001/2002: £7,500
2002/2003: £7,700
2003/2004: £7,900
2004/2005: £8,200

Example ("George the Fifth")

George has a capital gain of £128,926 in 2004/2005, after claiming all relevant reliefs, including Taper Relief. After setting off his annual exemption of £8,200, he will be left with a taxable gain of £120,726.

Note: in this example, and in the one in section 4.20 below, we have assumed that the annual exemption is fully available. This will not always be the case and it should be remembered that the exemption applies to all of an individual's capital gains, net of capital losses, for a whole tax year, and not specifically to any single gain.

4.20 The Amount of Tax Payable

Having arrived at the taxable gain, it only remains to work out how much tax is actually payable.

Capital Gains Tax is calculated at the same rate as would have applied if the taxable gain had been an extra slice of interest income received by the taxpayer in the same tax year on top of all other income (including dividends and their related tax credits). (See section 3.3 and Appendix A for further details of tax rates and their application.)

Hence, if the taxpayer is already a higher rate taxpayer for Income Tax purposes, Capital Gains Tax will be paid at a flat rate of 40%.

For an individual with no taxable income whatsoever in the same tax year, the Capital Gains Tax would be calculated as follows (based on 2004/2005 rates):

- On the first £2,020: 10%
- On the next £29,380: 20% (the "savings rate")
- On the remainder: 40%

Of course, many taxpayers are in a position somewhere between these two extremes. For these individuals, the amount of Capital Gains Tax payable is calculated by first using up what remains of their lower and basic rate tax bands (£31,400 in total) and then taxing any remaining amount at the higher rate, 40%

Example ("George the Sixth")

George has a taxable gain for 2004/2005, after all reliefs and exemptions, of £120,726. His gross income for 2004/2005 totals £12,000. After deducting his personal Income Tax allowance for 2004/2005 (£4,745) this leaves him with taxable income of £7,255.

George therefore pays Capital Gains Tax as follows:

- Nil at 10% (his lower rate band has already been fully used up by income).
- £24,145 at 20% (the amount of his basic rate tax band still available after the amount used up by income - £31,400 LESS £7,255) = £4,829.
- £96,581 at 40% (the remainder of the gain - £120,726 LESS £24,145) = £38,632.

Total Capital Gains Tax payable: £43,461.

4.21 When is Capital Gains Tax Payable?

The total amount of Capital Gains Tax payable for each tax year is due and payable by 31st January following the end of the tax year. Hence, in the example in section 4.20 above, George's Capital Gains Tax liability of £43,461 for 2004/2005 is due by 31st January 2006.

Capital Gains Tax liabilities are excluded from the instalment system applying to Income Tax liabilities under self assessment (see section 3.2).

4.22 What Must I Report to the Inland Revenue?

For tax years up to and including 2002/2003, any capital disposal, other than one which:

a) was wholly covered by the principal private residence exemption alone, or

b) which did not give rise to proceeds (or "deemed proceeds" – see section 4.6) of more than twice the annual exemption and which also did not produce a capital gain in excess of the annual exemption,

had to be reported on pages CG1 to CG8 of the tax return (the Capital Gains Supplement).

For tax years from 2003/2004 onwards, the reporting requirements have been relaxed slightly so that, broadly, only disposals giving rise to proceeds exceeding four times the annual exemption, or which do give rise to an actual Capital Gains Tax liability, will need to be reported. Unfortunately, in practice, this is unlikely to eliminate many property disposals from the requirement to make a tax return.

Disposals which are fully covered by the principal private residence exemption alone continue to be exempted from reporting requirements. This includes cases where the "last three years of ownership" rule applies to fully exempt the gain, but does not include cases where the taxpayer is additionally relying on the private letting exemption to ensure full relief from Capital Gains Tax.

The Return is due for submission by 31st January following the end of the relevant tax year (i.e. by the same date that any Capital Gains Tax liability is due).

Pages CG1 to CG8 form the Capital Gains Supplement of the tax return and can be obtained by calling the Revenue's own order line, 0845 9000 404 or by downloading them from www.inlandrevenue.gov.uk.

4.23 Jointly Held Assets

Where two or more taxpayers hold assets jointly, they must each calculate their own Capital Gains Tax based on their own share of the net proceeds received less their own base cost.

Example

Taking the same facts as the example used in sections 4.6 to 4.20 above ("George"), except that the house is held jointly with his wife, Charlotte. Charlotte's income for 2004/2005 is less than her personal Income Tax allowance (£4,745).

Up to the point of calculating the tapered gain (section 4.15), everything will be exactly the same, except that George and Charlotte will each have a gain of exactly half of the amount given for George. The major changes will come in the fact that each of them has their own annual exemption and each will be subject to different tax rates. This can be summarised as follows:

	£
Net proceeds	184,475 (half of £368,950 – section 4.6)
Less:	
Base Cost	72,525 (half of £145,050 – section 4.7)
Indexation	25,999 (half of £51,998 – section 4.9)
Equals:	85,951
Less:	
Taper relief (25%, as before)	21,488
Equals:	64,463
Less:	
Annual Exemption	8,200
Equals:	56,263

Tax Payable

Based on the same facts as in "George the Sixth" in section 4.20 above, George would pay Capital Gains Tax on his gain as follows:

- £24,145 at 20% (as before, the amount of his basic rate tax band still available after the amount used up by income - £31,400 LESS £7,255) = £4,829.
- £32,118 at 40% (the remainder of George's gain - £56,263 LESS £24,145) = £12,847.

George's Capital Gains Tax bill: £17,676.

Having no taxable income for the year, Charlotte will pay Capital Gains Tax as follows:
- £2,020 at 10%   = £202
- £29,380 at 20%   = £5,876
- £24,863 at 40% (£56,263 LESS £31,400) = £9,945

Charlotte's Capital Gains Tax bill: £16,023

It is well worth noting that the total Capital Gains Tax now payable by the couple, £33,699, is considerably less than the amount George had to pay when he owned the house in his sole name (£43,461 – see section 4.20 above).

Another important point to note when looking at jointly held property is that the £40,000 limit for Private Letting Relief (see section 4.11) applies to each individual taxpayer. Hence, up to a total of £80,000 can be exempted by that relief where a house is held jointly by a married couple. We will examine the potential effect of this later in Chapter Six.

4.24 Capital Losses

Generally speaking, capital losses are computed in the same way as capital gains. However, there are a few significant differences in the treatment of capital losses, as follows:

a) When dealing with the base cost of assets acquired before 31st March 1982 (section 4.8), the question of whether to use the March 1982 value or the original cost is determined according to whichever produces the lower loss. If one produces a loss and the other a gain, then a "no gain/no loss" disposal results.

b) Indexation relief (section 4.9) cannot augment or create a capital loss. Hence, where there is a capital loss before indexation relief, no indexation relief is given. In other cases, indexation relief must be limited to a maximum equivalent to the amount that would bring the gain after indexation relief down to nil.

c) Taper relief does not apply to capital losses.

d) Where a taxpayer has an overall net capital loss for the year, it is carried forward and set off against gains in future years BUT only to the extent necessary to reduce future gains down to the annual exemption applying for that future year.

e) Capital losses arising on any transactions with "connected persons" (see section 4.6) may only be set off against gains arising on transactions between the same parties.

4.25 Leases

The taxation treatment of leases has a long and chequered history. Here is a brief summary of the current situation.

4.25.1 Granting a long lease of more than 50 years' duration

This is a capital disposal, fully chargeable to Capital Gains Tax (subject to applicable reliefs). The Base Cost to be used has to be restricted under the "part disposal" rules. In essence, what this means is that the Base Cost is divided between the part disposed of (i.e. the lease) and the part retained (the "reversionary interest") in proportion to their relative values.

Example

Llewellyn owns the freehold of a commercial property in Cardiff. He grants a 60 years lease to Brian, a businessman from Belfast moving into the area. Brian pays a premium of £90,000 for the *lease. The value of Llewellyn's reversionary interest is established as £10,000.*

The Base Cost to be used in calculating Llewellyn's capital gain on the grant of the lease is therefore 90% of his Base Cost for the property as a whole.

4.25.2 Granting a short lease of no more than 50 years' duration

As already explained in section 3.14, part of any lease premium obtained will be taxable as income. The remainder is a capital disposal and is dealt with in the same way as outlined in 4.25.1 above.

4.25.3 Assigning a long lease with no less than 50 years' duration remaining

This is simply a straightforward capital disposal. Any applicable reliefs may be claimed in the usual way.

4.25.4 Assigning a short lease with less than 50 years' duration remaining

This is treated entirely as a capital disposal. However, leases with less than 50 years remaining are treated as "wasting assets". The taxpayer is therefore required to reduce his Base Cost in accordance with a schedule contained in tax legislation. For example, for a lease with 20 years remaining, and which had more than 50 years remaining when first acquired, the Base Cost must be reduced to 72.77% of the original amount.

Chapter 5

Other Taxes to Watch Out For

5.1 Stamp Duty - Introduction

Stamp Duty is the oldest tax on the statute books. It was several centuries old already when Pitt the Younger introduced Income Tax in 1799. Even today, we are still governed (to a limited extent) by the Stamp Act 1891.

From 1st December 2003, however, for transfers of real property (i.e. land and buildings, or any form of legal interest in them), Stamp Duty has been replaced by Stamp Duty Land Tax.

5.2 Stamp Duty Land Tax

On 1st December 2003, the new 'Stamp Duty Land Tax' came into force for transfers of real property (i.e. land and buildings or any form of legal interest in them).

The rates of Stamp Duty Land Tax applying to transfers of property are the same regardless of what type of property business the purchaser has and regardless of whether that purchaser is an individual, a trust, a partnership or a company.

Unfortunately, the introduction of the new tax has mainly preserved the dramatic increases in the rates of Stamp Duty that we have seen over the last few years. Stamp Duty has been at the forefront of Gordon Brown's strategy of 'stealth taxation', through which he has raised additional taxes in ways which largely go unnoticed in the media frenzy that surrounds the annual Budget process. The changeover to the Stamp Duty Land Tax regime has done nothing to alter this and, for larger transactions, the tax still represents a significant barrier to property investment.

The rates of Stamp Duty Land Tax (other than in 'disadvantaged areas' – see below) are as follows:

- Residential property up to £60,000 – Zero.

- Non-residential property up to £150,000 – Zero.

- Residential property over £60,000 but not more than £250,000 – 1%.

- Non-residential property over £150,000 but not more than £250,000 – 1%.

- All property over £250,000 but not more than £500,000 – 3%.

- All property over £500,000 – 4%.

All of the amounts indicated above refer to the consideration paid for the purchase – whether in cash or by any other means.

Like Stamp Duty, the Stamp Duty Land Tax payable is always rounded up to the nearest £5.

Whenever any rate less than the maximum 4% is to be applied, the purchaser is required to certify that the lower rate is properly applicable. A new, complex, and very lengthy form has been introduced for this purpose!

Furthermore, it should also be noted that the rate of Stamp Duty Land Tax to be applied must be determined after taking account of any 'associated transactions' taking place.

It can readily be seen from the above table that a small alteration in the purchase price of a property can sometimes make an enormous difference to the amount of Stamp Duty Land Tax payable.

Example

Ian is just about to make an offer of £250,001 for a house in Edinburgh when he realises that the Stamp Duty Land Tax payable on this purchase, at 3%, would be £7,505. Horrified at this prospect, he amends the offer to £249,999, thus reducing the potential Stamp Duty Land Tax payable to £2,500 (1%).

This sort of change is, of course, perfectly acceptable, because the whole situation is taking place at 'arm's-length'.

However, where connected parties are involved, the Inland Revenue's Stamp Office is likely to scrutinise very closely any transactions where the consideration is only just under one of the limits set out above.

Leases

Stamp Duty Land Tax is also payable on leases (sometimes known as 'Lease Duty') and this represents one of the most significant changes from the old Stamp Duty regime. (Although Stamp Duty was often payable on leases under the old regime, it had some rather odd quirks and was open to a good deal of abuse.)

The Stamp Duty Land Tax payable on the granting of a lease is based on the 'Net Present Value' of all of the rent payable under the lease over its entire term. Where the net present value does not exceed £60,000 (for residential property) or £150,000 (for non-residential property), no Stamp Duty Land Tax will be payable. For new leases with a net present value exceeding these limits, Stamp Duty Land Tax is payable at a rate of 1% on the excess.

VAT is excluded from the rent payable under the lease for the purposes of Stamp Duty Land Tax calculations <u>unless</u> the landlord has already exercised the option to tax (this applies to commercial property only). (Previously, under the Stamp Duty regime, there was an assumption that VAT should be included in such calculations for commercial property leases, unless the lease specifically prohibited the charging of VAT.)

Example

Clive is about to take on a 10-year lease over a house in Kent at an annual rent of £12,000.

The 'Net Present Value' of the first year's rent is simply £12,000.

The second year's rent, however, has a lower 'Net Present Value' because it is not payable for 12 months. The Stamp Duty Land Tax legislation provides that the net present value of a sum of money due in 12 months' time is equal to the sum due divided by a 'discount factor'. The applicable discount factor is currently 103.5%.

Hence, the 'Present Value' of a sum of £12,000 due in 12 months' time is only £11,594 (i.e. £12,000 divided by 103.5%).

Similarly, the third year's rent, which is due a further twelve months later, must be 'discounted' again by the same amount, i.e. £11,594/103.5% = £11,202.

This process is continued for the entire 10-year life of the lease and the net present values of all of the rental payments are than added together to give the total net present value for the whole lease. In this case, this works out at £103,292.

The Stamp Duty Land Tax payable by Clive is therefore £435 (1% of £103,292 less £60,000, £43,292, rounded up to the nearest £5).

Note that it does not matter for the purposes of this calculation whether the rent is payable monthly, quarterly or annually, or whether it is payable in advance or in arrears. Net present value is, in each case, always calculated by reference to the total annual rental payable for each year of the lease.

The current 'discount factor' (103.5%) may be changed in the future, depending on a number of factors, including the prevailing rates of inflation and interest.

Lease Premiums

Lease **premiums** also attract Stamp Duty Land Tax at the same rates as given above for outright purchases. (Special rules apply where there is also annual gross rent payable in excess of £600.)

Disadvantaged Areas

There are 2,000 areas in the UK that have been specifically designated as 'Disadvantaged Areas'. This is done by reference to postcodes in England and Wales and by reference to Electoral Wards in Scotland. (My apologies to readers with properties in Northern Ireland – I don't know how it is done there.)

These areas are sometimes also known as 'Enterprise Neighbourhoods' or 'Enterprise Areas' and, in fact, very often are not really all that 'disadvantaged' at all – so don't be fooled by the name.

A number of tax reliefs have been introduced to assist development in these areas, including some significant relaxations in the amount of Stamp Duty Land Tax payable on properties in these areas.

Residential properties within these areas are subject to the zero rate of Stamp Duty Land Tax on purchases where the consideration does not exceed £150,000.

Non-residential properties within these areas are fully exempt from Stamp Duty Land Tax.

Application to all UK Property

Stamp Duty Land Tax is payable on all transfers of UK property in accordance with the above rules regardless of where the vendor or purchaser are resident and regardless of where the transfer documentation is drawn up.

5.3 Stamp Duty on Shares

Before we leave the subject of Stamp Duty (or Stamp Duty Land Tax), it is just worth briefly mentioning that the rate of Stamp Duty on purchases of shares and securities is still unchanged at a single uniform rate of only 0.5%.

This has led to many tax-avoidance strategies, designed to avoid the excessive rates applied to property transactions by making use of this more palatable rate. However, new legislation introduced by both the 2002 and 2003 Budgets has effectively blocked most of the more popular methods.

Nevertheless, for those investing in property through a company, there remains the possibility of selling shares in that company at a much lower rate of Duty than would apply to the sale of individual properties within the company.

5.4 Inheritance Tax

Inheritance Tax is the direct descendant of Estate Duty and Capital Transfer Tax. It is quite ironic that Inheritance Tax should have such a long lineage because it is, of course, one's descendants who will suffer its effects.

Inheritance Tax is really a complete subject in its own right. For a full examination of the workings of this tax and the planning opportunities available to reduce its potential impact on your family see the Taxcafe.co.uk guide *How to Avoid Inheritance Tax*.

Nevertheless, death and taxes are, of course, the only two certainties in life and unless pre-emptive action is taken, sooner or later an Inheritance Tax liability will arise whenever a UK domiciled individual owns property worth more than the "Nil Rate Band". It is therefore worth us taking a brief look at the potential impact of this tax.

If you are UK domiciled then, on your death, Inheritance Tax will be levied at one single rate of 40% on the entire value of your estate, less certain exemptions. The first, and for most people perhaps the most important, exemption is the Nil Rate Band. As the name suggests, this means that an Inheritance Tax rate of nil is applied to the first part of your estate, which falls within this band. From 6th April 2004, the Nil Rate Band will stand at £263,000.

Example

Amjeed has spent many years building up a property portfolio. At the time of his death in December 2004, his portfolio is worth £2,000,000. He has no other assets and no liabilities.

The first £263,000 of Amjeed's estate is exempt from Inheritance Tax, as it is covered by the Nil Rate Band. The remaining £1,737,000, however, is charged to Inheritance Tax at 40%, giving rise to a tax charge of £694,800!

In certain circumstances, Inheritance Tax can also apply to transfers of assets (or cash) made during a person's lifetime. However, for most people, death is the only occasion when they (or, more accurately, their executors), are concerned with this tax.

Apart from the Nil Rate Band, there are a number of other Inheritance Tax exemptions and reliefs available. The most important of these is probably the fact that transfers to spouses are wholly exempt (unless they are foreign domiciled, when the exemption is restricted to £55,000).

Domicile

Inheritance Tax is payable on the worldwide assets of UK domiciled individuals. Foreign domiciled individuals are only subject to Inheritance Tax on assets situated in the UK.

Under general principles, most people acquire their father's domicile at birth and hence your domicile is usually your country of birth (or his, if you were living abroad at the time). You can change your domicile, but it is difficult. An intention to stay abroad permanently is required.

Notwithstanding any of the above, anyone who has been resident in the UK for at least 17 out of the last 20 tax years is deemed to be UK domiciled for Inheritance Tax purposes. In some cases, this may be affected by a Double Tax Treaty between the UK and their country of origin.

The Implication of High Property Values

For the vast majority of people, the largest proportion of their estate will be property. Inheritance Tax was once viewed as a "rich man's tax", but recent dramatic increases in property values mean that even modestly wealthy people will find that, without careful planning, their estate has a large potential Inheritance Tax liability.

5.5 VAT

VAT, or 'Value Added Tax', to give it its proper name, is the 'new kid on the block' in UK taxation terms, having arrived on our shores from Europe on 1 January 1973.

Despite its youth, VAT is, quite probably, the UK's most hated tax and there are some nasty pitfalls awaiting the unwary property investor at the hands of this indirect form of taxation.

Unlike all of the other taxes mentioned so far in this guide, VAT is administered and collected by Her Majesty's Customs & Excise, rather than the Inland Revenue. (Although the two departments are due to merge in the near future.)

Residential Property Letting

Generally speaking, a property investment business, engaged primarily in residential property letting, does not need to be registered for VAT. (Nor, indeed, very often would it be able to.)

The letting of residential property is an exempt supply for VAT purposes. VAT is therefore not chargeable on rent, although, of course, VAT cannot be recovered on expenses and the landlord should therefore claim VAT-inclusive costs for Income Tax and Capital Gains Tax purposes.

Beware, however, that the provision of ancillary services (e.g. cleaning or gardening) may sometimes be Standard-Rated, and hence subject to VAT at 17.5%, if the value of annual supplies of these services exceeds the registration threshold, (£58,000 from 1st April 2004).

Some landlords making ancillary supplies of this nature prefer to register for VAT, even if they have not reached the registration threshold, as this means that they are able to recover some of the VAT on their expenses.

Commercial Property Letting

For commercial property, there is an 'option to tax'. In other words, the landlord may choose, for each property (on a property-by-property basis), whether or not the rent should be an exempt supply for VAT purposes.

If the 'option to tax' is exercised, the rent on the property becomes Standard Rated (at 17.5%) for VAT purposes. The landlord may then recover VAT on all of the expenses relating to that property.

Ancillary services are again likely to be Standard Rated if supplies exceed the registration threshold.

Tax Tip

If the potential tenants of a commercial property are all, or mostly, likely to be VAT-registered businesses themselves, it will generally make sense to exercise the 'option to tax' on the property in order to recover the VAT on expenses incurred.

Property Sales

Sales of newly constructed residential property are zero-rated for VAT purposes. This means that the developer can recover all of the VAT on their construction costs without having to charge VAT on the sale of the property. (In theory, VAT is charged, but at a rate of zero.)

This treatment is extended to the sale of a property which has just been converted from a non-residential property into a residential property (e.g. converting a barn into a house).

It is also extended to 'substantially reconstructed protected buildings'. I will leave Customs & Excise to explain what that means!

Other sales of residential property are generally an exempt supply meaning, once again, that the taxpayer making the sale is unable to recover any of the VAT on his or her expenses.

Where the 'option to tax' has previously been exercised on a commercial property, the sale of that property will again be Standard Rated and this has major implications for such transactions.

Sales of new or uncompleted commercial property are Standard Rated for VAT purposes.

Property Management

Property management services are Standard Rated for VAT and hence a property management business will need to be registered for VAT if its annual supplies (i.e. sales) exceed the £58,000 registration threshold. The taxpayer may still register voluntarily even if the level of sales is below the threshold.

Whether the properties under management are residential or commercial makes no difference for this purpose.

Naturally, a property management business that is registered for VAT can recover the VAT on most of its business expenses. There are, however, a few exceptions where VAT cannot be wholly recovered (*e.g. on the purchase of motor cars*).

Interaction with Income Tax and Capital Gains Tax

Any business that is registered for VAT should generally include only the net (i.e. excluding VAT) amounts of income and expenditure in its accounts. Where VAT recovery is barred or restricted (*e.g. on the provision of private fuel for proprietors or staff*), however, the additional cost arising may generally be claimed as an expense for Income Tax purposes.

A non-registered business should include the VAT in its business expenditure for Income Tax purposes.

Similar principles apply for Capital Gains Tax purposes.

5.6 National Insurance Contributions

In most cases, rental income is not classed as "earnings" and is not therefore subject to National Insurance Contributions.

In a few instances, individual taxpayers with income from furnished holiday lettings have been charged for Class 2 National Insurance Contributions. The Class 2 rate is, however, only £2.05 per week for 2004/2005.

All forms of letting income are specifically exempted from the rather more significant Class 4 National Insurance Contributions.

For 2004/2005, Class 4 National Insurance Contributions will be charged at 8% on earnings between £4,745 and £31,720 per annum and at 1% on all earnings over £31,720.

Taxpayers can, of course, pay voluntary Class 3 National Insurance Contributions of £7.15 per week in order to secure state retirement benefits, etc, if they so wish.

Naturally, if you should employ anyone to help you in your property business, then their salary will be subject to both employer's and employee's Class 1 National Insurance Contributions (at 11% and 12.8% respectively). If you provide them with any taxable Benefits-in-Kind, you will additionally be liable for Class 1A National Insurance Contributions (again at 12.8%).

Property Trades

If your property business is classed as a "trade" (see Chapter Two), you will be liable for both Class 2 and Class 4 National Insurance Contributions on your profits.

This has the result of giving you overall effective tax rates (combining Income Tax and National Insurance Contributions) as follows:

- Profits up to £4,745:   Nil
- Profits between £4,745 and £6,765:   18%
- Profits between £6,765 and £31,720:   30%
- Profits between £31,720 and £36,145:   23%
- Profits over £36,145:   41%

Plus, in most cases, an additional £109 in Class 2 National Insurance Contributions.

(Note the rather odd quirk of the reduced rate between £31,720 and £36,145!)

Capital Gains

National Insurance Contributions are never payable on capital gains.

Remember, however, that if you are classed as a property developer or a property trader, your profit on property sales will be taxed as income and hence will be subject to National Insurance Contributions.

Chapter 6

Advanced Tax Planning

6.1 Introduction to Tax Planning

In the first five chapters we have looked at the mechanics of the UK tax system as it applies to the individual property investor. A great many planning ideas and principles have already emerged and doubtless, by now, some readers will have begun to form ideas of their own.

In this chapter we will take a look at some further useful planning strategies for property investors. These strategies relate in the main to those investors who continue to hold their property investments personally.

In many cases, the best tax planning results will be obtained through the use of a combination of different techniques, rather than merely following any single one. Each situation is different and the optimum solution only comes through a detailed analysis of all the relevant facts.

Tax planning should therefore never be undertaken without full knowledge of the facts of the case and the exact circumstances of the individuals and other legal entities involved.

For this reason, the techniques laid out in this chapter, which are by no means exhaustive, are intended only to give you some idea of the tax savings which can be achieved through careful planning. If and when you come to undertake any tax planning measures of your own you should seek professional advice from someone fully acquainted with your own situation. The author cannot accept any responsibility for any action taken, or any decision made to refrain from action, by any readers of this guide.

So, that's the health warning, now for the interesting stuff....

6.2 Using Your Spouse

Your spouse has a number of uses. Some of them relate to taxation.

Putting property into joint names with your spouse can generate both Income Tax and Capital Gains Tax savings. The transfer itself is free from tax and does not result in any loss of reliefs.

The example in section 4.23 above (George and Charlotte), already demonstrates the potential Capital Gains Tax savings. However, it is immaterial whether the property was in joint ownership throughout, or was only transferred into joint ownership at a later date, prior to the ultimate sale. The effect on the couple's final tax liabilities remains exactly the same.

Furthermore, where there is scope to claim the private letting exemption, it is possible to double the maximum amount of relief available (from £40,000 to £80,000) by putting the property into joint names prior to sale.

Two key provisos must be made here however:

i)   The spouse must be beneficially entitled to his/her share of the sale proceeds. Any attempt to prevent this could make the transfer invalid for tax purposes.

ii)   An interim transfer of property into joint names prior to sale must take place early enough to ensure that the spouse genuinely has beneficial title to their share. If it is left until the ultimate sale is a contractual certainty, it may be too late to be effective for tax purposes.

It should also be noted that a transfer into joint names prior to sale is not always beneficial. Sometimes, it is preferable to have the property in the sole name of one spouse at the time of sale. This situation is likely to arise, for example, if:

a) One spouse is a higher rate taxpayer, whilst the other has little or no income,

    b) One spouse's annual exemption for Capital Gains Tax will be fully or partly utilised on other capital gains in the same year, whilst the other spouse's annual exemption remains fully available, or

    c) One spouse has capital losses available to set off against the gain on the property.

If the best spouse to hold the property at the time of the sale is not the one that already holds it then a pre-sale transfer could generate considerable savings. The same provisos as set out above apply equally here.

In summary, when a sale is in prospect, it is well worth assessing whether a transfer into joint ownership, or to the other spouse outright, might result in a significant Capital Gains Tax saving. Always remember, however, that whoever has legal title to the property at the time of the sale is entitled to the proceeds!

6.3 Have Your Cake and Eat it

Income Tax savings can also be generated by transferring an investment property into either joint names with your spouse or into the sole name of the spouse with a lower overall income.

In the right circumstances, moving income from one spouse to another in this way can save up to almost £8,000 in Income Tax *each year* (based on 2004/2005 tax rates).

However, as explained in section 6.2 above, this form of tax planning is not effective unless beneficial title in the property is genuinely transferred to the spouse. But not everyone trusts their spouse enough to simply hand over the title to their property (or half of it)!

For Income Tax purposes at least, there is a way to solve this dilemma. Where property is held jointly by husband and wife, there is an automatic presumption, for Income Tax purposes, that the income arises in equal shares. This 50/50 split will continue to be applied unless and until the couple jointly elect for the income to be split in accordance with the true beneficial title in the property.

Hence, where a married property owner wants to save Income Tax on their rental profits without giving up too much of their title to the property, what they should do is:

- Transfer the property into joint names with their spouse.
- Retain 99% of the beneficial ownership and transfer only 1% to the spouse.
  AND
- Simply never elect for the income to be split in accordance with the true beneficial title.

6.4 Climbing the Ladder

In section 4.11 we saw just how far the principal private residence exemption can be extended through its interaction with other reliefs.

This can be used to great effect to enable a taxpayer to build up a property portfolio virtually free of any Capital Gains Tax. The basic method is best explained by way of example.

Example 6.4.1

Malcolm buys a small flat (Flat A) in 2002. He moves in and it becomes his main residence. A year after buying the first flat, he buys another, larger, flat (Flat B). He does not immediately move into the new flat but spends a year renovating it. He moves into Flat B in 2004, just before the anniversary of its purchase and then starts renting out Flat A as private residential accommodation.

The story so far

Malcolm now has two flats, both of which will be fully exempted by the principal private residence exemption until at least 2007. The private letting exemption may also further extend Flat A's tax free status until at least 2012 (depending on the ultimate sale price).

Example 6.4.2

In 2005, Malcolm buys a house (House C). Again, he does not move in immediately but spends a year renovating the house before moving in just before the anniversary of its purchase.

He now starts renting out Flat B as private residential accommodation.

The story so far (2006)

Flat A is likely to be exempt from any Capital Gains Tax until at least 2012, Flat B will be fully exempted until at least 2009 and quite possibly until 2015 and House C will be fully exempted until at least 2009, possibly 2013. All of this without even resorting to taper relief or the annual exemption.

You get the idea!

Eventually some of the earlier acquisitions will begin to be exposed to Capital Gains Tax. As illustrated in section 4.11, however, this may take several years. When that point is reached, Malcolm can sell off the properties one at a time in order to make best use of his annual exemptions.

Potential Drawbacks

The first and most obvious potential problem is finance. However, with the rapid expansion in the "buy-to-let" mortgage market it would seem feasible for someone to follow a strategy similar to Malcolm's.

Secondly, the Inland Revenue have the power to overturn the principal private residence exemption if they perceive that the taxpayer is carrying on a trade of property development or is acquiring properties with no motive other than to realise a profit. Hence, Malcolm's strategy does carry a degree of risk and certainly would be unlikely to succeed beyond the first few properties.

Relying On The principal private residence Exemption

In this, as with any other planning scenario which places reliance on the principal private residence exemption, it is essential to ensure that the property or properties concerned genuinely become your private residence.

There is no "hard and fast" rule as to how long you must reside in a property to establish it as your private residence for Capital

Gains Tax purposes. It is the quality of occupation that counts, not the length. Hence, it is recommended that:

i)   You (and your spouse &/or family, if applicable), move into the property for a substantial period.

ii)   You ensure that all relevant institutions (banks, utilities, the Inland Revenue, etc) are notified that the property is your new, permanent, address.

iii)   You inform family and friends that this address is your new permanent home.

iv)   You furnish the property for permanent occupation.

v)   You register on the electoral roll for that address.

vi)   You do not advertise the property for sale or rent until after the expiry of a substantial period.

It is not possible to provide a definitive view of what would constitute a "substantial period". What matters is that the property genuinely becomes your "permanent home" for a period. In this context, "permanent" means "not temporary", i.e. intended to be your residence, rather than a temporary abode. You must move into the property with no clear plans for moving out again.

As a rough guide only, you should plan your affairs on the basis that you will be residing in the property for at least a year. However, as already stated, the question would ultimately be decided on quality of occupation, rather than length. Where you are looking to use the principal private residence exemption on a property you must embark upon occupying that property completely wholeheartedly; a mere "sham" occupation will not suffice.

In some instances, you may be able to establish the desired result merely by electing for the property to be treated as your main residence (see section 4.12.7). However, it can only be your main residence if it is indeed your private residence and the safest way to ensure that a property is accepted as being your private residence, is to make it your main residence, or even your only residence, by following the measures set out above.

6.5 General Elections

As explained in section 4.12.7, where a taxpayer has two or more private residences it is possible to elect which is to be regarded as their main residence. In fact, it is more than possible, it is highly advisable, even when it seems obvious which property should be regarded as the main residence.

Example 6.5.1

Diana owns a house in London purchased in 1999 for £300,000. In 2002, she buys a small cottage in Sussex for £100,000, to be used as her "weekend retreat", although, in fact, she only manages to spend a few weekends a year there.

In 2006, plans for a new motorway junction to be built only half a mile from Diana's cottage are announced. Simultaneously, the value of her property increases dramatically due to the demand for industrial units in the area, whilst her own desire to use the place herself rapidly diminishes. A few months later, she sells it for an astonishing £400,000.

Now, fortunately for Diana, her accountant had insisted that she make a main residence election in 2003. At the time, she naturally elected that her London house was her main residence, since it seemed far more likely to produce a significant capital gain.

Because of this earlier election, however, Diana was able to make a new election in 2006, stipulating her Sussex cottage as her main residence. As a result, the cottage is covered by the principal private residence exemption for the last three years of Diana's ownership, thus exempting her from Capital Gains Tax on £225,000 out of her total gain of £300,000, a saving of up to £90,000!

Furthermore, her London house will only lose its principal private residence exempt status for the short period from the date of Diana's new election to the date of sale of her cottage.

The moral of the story – always, always, always make the main residence election where applicable.

Tax Tip

A property only has to be classed as your main residence for **any** period, no matter how short, in order for your last three years of ownership to be exempted under the principal private residence exemption.

Hence, in order to minimise the impact on the principal private residence relief available to another property, it is only necessary to elect in favour of the new "main residence" for a very short period.

In Diana's case, she could have preserved most of the principal private residence exemption on her London house by making another revised "main residence" election in favour of that property a week after she had made the election in favour of her Sussex cottage.

Wealth Warning

Electing for a residence to be your "main residence" for just a week is fine.

Do not confuse this, however, with the need to establish the property as being your private residence in the first place (as explained in section 6.4 above), where a considerably longer period of occupation is recommended.

6.6 Something in the Garden

It's a common scenario: a taxpayer has a large garden so he sells part of it off for property development. (See section 4.12 above for general guidance on the limitations of the principal private residence exemption in these circumstances).

There are the right ways to do this and there are other ways, which are very, very wrong.

The wrong ways

DO NOT:

- Sell your house first before selling the development plot.

- Fence the development plot off or otherwise separate it from the rest of your garden before selling it.

- Use the development plot for any purpose other than your own private residential occupation immediately prior to the sale.

Each of these will result in the complete loss of your principal private residence exemption for the development plot.

And, furthermore, do not assume that the plot is covered by the principal private residence exemption if the total area of your garden exceeds half a hectare.

The right ways

First, the simple way:

Carefully ensuring that you do not commit any of the cardinal sins described above, you simply sell off the plot of land. This sale will now enjoy the same principal private residence exemption as applies to your house itself, whether that be full or partial. (E.g., if 90% of a gain on your house would have been exempt, then 90% of the gain on the plot of land will be exempt.)

The other "right way"

The only drawback to the simple way is that you do not get to participate in any of the profit on the development of the plot.

But, what if you hang on to the plot and develop it yourself?

Yes, at first this looks like we've gone the wrong way, but not if you then proceed to move into the new property and adopt it as your main residence.

Your old house can safely be sold at any time up to three years after the date you move out and still be covered by the principal private residence exemption.

The new house should be fully covered by the principal private residence exemption as long as you moved in within a year of the date that development started.

As in section 6.4, there are some potential dangers here, but the exemption should be available if you genuinely adopt the new house as your new main residence.

6.7 Student Loans

Each unmarried individual is entitled to have their own main private residence which is exempt from Capital Gains Tax. Once your children reach the age of 18 therefore, it is possible to put some tax-free capital growth into their hands. (They do not actually have to be students by the way – it works just as well if they are in employment or even just living a life of leisure at your expense, as many teenagers seem to do!)

The method is fairly straightforward, all that you need to do is purchase a property in their name which they then move into and adopt as their main residence.

Financing can be achieved in a number of ways, but the important point is that they must have legal and beneficial title to the property. (Hence this technique should only be undertaken if you are prepared to pass wealth on to the children.)

The purchase of the property has possible Inheritance Tax implications but these are avoided simply by surviving for seven years.

6.8 Multiple Exemptions

This method looks fairly clumsy, but can save some reasonably large amounts of Capital Gains Tax. It simply revolves around using a transfer of property into joint names with a friend or family member, and a short delay in the ultimate sale, to triple the number of annual exemptions available and double the potential to utilise the lower and basic rate tax bands.

Again, it is best illustrated by way of an example. All figures quoted in this example are based on 2004/2005 tax rates and on the assumption that a half share in a property is worth 90% of half of the value of the whole property.

Example 6.8.1

Edmund has a property which he is looking to sell in the near future. He anticipates making a capital gain of £150,000 after all available exemptions other than his annual exemption. He has only a modest level of income, below the level of his personal allowance. A straightforward sale now would nevertheless still give him a Capital Gains Tax liability of £50,238.

What Edmund does, however, is to put the property into joint names with his adult son, Edgar, as "tenants in common". This still gives him a Capital Gains Tax liability, as he has made a disposal to a connected person and this must be treated as having taken place at market value.

However, he has only disposed of a half share in the property, which, as "tenants in common" is only worth 90% of half of what the whole property is worth, so his immediate Capital Gains Tax liability is only £17,238.

In the following tax year, Edmund and Edgar sell their jointly owned property. Edmund has another Capital Gains Tax liability of £20,238. Edgar's modest gain is covered by his annual exemption.

The total Capital Gains Tax payable by Edmund amounts to £37,476 and a saving of £12,762 has therefore been achieved.

As in section 6.7 above, this technique may involve the passing on of wealth and again has possible Inheritance Tax implications. As with other methods described it is also essential that beneficial title in the property is genuinely passed over.

6.9 Reinvestment Reliefs

6.9.1 Venture Capital Trusts

Until 5th April 2004, a Capital Gains Tax liability may be deferred by reinvesting some or all of the underlying untapered capital gain in Venture Capital Trusts. The investment(s) must take place within a year (before or after) of the date of the disposal which gives rise to the gain.

A maximum of £100,000 may be invested in Venture Capital Trusts in any one tax year up to and including 2003/2004.

Unfortunately, from 6th April 2004, the ability to defer Capital Gains Tax through reinvestment of gains in Venture Capital Trusts will be withdrawn.

6.9.2 Enterprise Investment Scheme ("Enterprise Investment Scheme") Shares

Capital Gains Tax liabilities may also be deferred by reinvesting some or all of the underlying untapered capital gain in Enterprise Investment Scheme shares. In this case, the investment must take place within the period beginning a year before the date of the disposal which gave rise to the gain and ending three years after that date.

Enterprise Investment Scheme shares are not eligible for Income Tax relief (see 6.9.3) when the investor is connected with the company issuing the shares. However, this does not prevent reinvestment relief for Capital Gains Tax purposes from applying. Hence, a taxpayer could potentially defer Capital Gains Tax on his property gains by investing in his own company!

Unfortunately, however, property investment companies are not eligible to issue Enterprise Investment Scheme shares, as the company must carry on a qualifying trade. Property development or property management activities might, however, be sufficient to enable a company to qualify in many instances.

Alternatively, products are now available which enable taxpayers to utilise a "portfolio" approach when investing in these intrinsically risky investments. This does not totally eliminate the risk, but it certainly improves the odds!

Unlike Venture Capital Trusts, the ability to defer Capital Gains Tax by reinvesting gains in Enterprise Investment Scheme shares continues after 6th April 2004.

6.9.3 Income Tax Relief and Other Points

Investments in both Venture Capital Trusts and Enterprise Investment Scheme shares also carry an Income Tax credit of up to 20% of the amount invested. In the case of Venture Capital Trusts this will increase to 40% with effect from 6th April 2004 (at the same time as Capital Gains Tax deferral relief on Venture Capital Trust investments is withdrawn), for a period of two years.

Hence, for Enterprise Investment Scheme shares and for Venture Capital Trust investments made until 5th April 2004, there is the potential for total tax savings of up to 60% of the amount invested!

Both types of investment must be made in cash. Enterprise Investment Scheme shares must also be Ordinary Shares, as defined in tax legislation. An annual limit of £150,000 applies to the amount invested in Enterprise Investment Scheme shares which is eligible for Income Tax relief, increasing to £200,000 from 2004/2005 onwards.

> **Tax Tip**
>
> With careful timing, Enterprise Investment Scheme shares could be used to defer capital gains of up to £1,000,000, whilst still obtaining total Income Tax savings of £200,000 over a five year period.
>
> Whilst there is no limit on the amount which can be invested annually in Enterprise Investment Scheme shares for Capital Gains Tax deferral purposes, it should be borne in mind that the Income Tax savings are permanent (unless certain rules regarding the period of ownership and other matters are broken).

Hence sticking within the annual investment limit of £200,000 for Income Tax purposes, where possible, is likely to be highly beneficial.

Example

Jerry anticipates making a taxable capital gain (before taper relief) of £1,000,000 on 1st May 2005.

He could defer all of his potential Capital Gains Tax liability by reinvesting his gain in Enterprise Investment Scheme shares at any time between 1st May 2004 and 1st May 2008. However, it is only by timing his investments very carefully that he will be able to obtain the maximum Income Tax saving of £200,000 also.

To do this, Jerry needs to time his Enterprise Investment Scheme share purchases as follows:

- *£200,000 between 1st May 2004 and 5th April 2005*
- *£200,000 during the 2005/2006 tax year*
- *£200,000 during the 2006/2007 tax year*
- *£200,000 during the 2007/2008 tax year*
- *£200,000 between 6th April and 1st May 2008*

If Jerry had simply made his whole £1,000,000 Enterprise Investment Scheme share investment in 2005/2006, he would have achieved the same Capital Gains Tax deferral relief, but would have managed an Income Tax saving of only £40,000, rather than the maximum £200,000.

6.10 Emigration

Taxpayers facing substantial potential Capital Gains Tax liabilities often avoid them by emigrating. However, merely going on a World cruise for a year will not usually be sufficient, as it is necessary to become non-UK ordinarily resident, as well as non-UK resident.

This is a complex field of tax planning, which really requires a separate guide on its own. However, the key points worth noting are:

- Emigration must generally be permanent or at least long-term (usually at least 5 complete UK tax years).

- Disposals must be deferred until non-residence has been achieved.

- Limited return visits to the UK are permitted.

- Returning prematurely to the UK, to resume permanent residence here, may result in substantial Capital Gains Tax liabilities.

- It is essential to ensure that there is no risk of inadvertently becoming liable for some form of capital taxation elsewhere. (There is no point in "jumping out of the frying pan and into the fire!")

- The taxation of non-residents is currently under review (a new consultative document was published on 9th April 2003).

Shorter periods of absence abroad may sometimes be sufficient to avoid UK Capital Gains Tax by making use of the terms of a Double Tax Treaty between the UK and the new country of residence (e.g. Belgium). Detailed professional advice should be sought when adopting this type of strategy.

6.11 Pension Relief

A new system of tax relief for pension contributions was introduced with effect from 6th April 2002. The new system is known as "stakeholder pensions".

Previously, relief for pension contributions could only be claimed against so-called "earned" income (employment income or self-employment income from a trade). Profits from a property investment business were treated as non-pensionable, as indeed were dividends received.

Under the new stakeholder pension system, relief may be claimed on up to £3,600 of gross pension contributions per annum without the need for any "earned income". Basic rate tax relief (at 22%) is given at source, so that actual payments of £2,808, or £234 per month, equate to gross contributions of £3,600.

Higher rate tax relief is then given through the self assessment tax system.

This is good news for property investors, for whom a measure of pension relief is now available for the first time.

Yet another major overhaul of the pension system is planned for implementation on 6th April 2006!

6.12 Using a Property Company to Save Tax

Many UK property investors are being increasingly drawn towards the idea of running their property business through a limited company.

Unlike other types of business, this does not generally appear to be due to the perceived protection afforded by a company's limited liability status. (In any case, limited liability status can now also be achieved through the medium of a Limited Liability Partnership.)

No, this decision appears to be entirely tax-driven and is a direct result of the current highly favourable Corporation Tax regime, especially the new "nil rate" of Corporation Tax introduced on 1st April 2002, which generally applies to the first £10,000 of a company's profits.

In arriving at its tax liability, a company's income and capital gains are simply aggregated together and then treated as one single total sum chargeable to Corporation Tax at effective rates varying from Zero to 32.75%, depending on the size of the company. These rates are almost always more beneficial than the corresponding marginal Income Tax rates payable by an individual on the same level of income, providing the opportunity to make huge annual tax savings on rental profits.

Conversely, however, a company does not have as many reliefs available under the capital gains regime and is not entitled to principal private residence relief, taper relief or an annual exemption.

Furthermore, there is a significant "catch" which lies in the fact that further tax costs will often arise when extracting profits or sale proceeds from the company. From 1st April 2004, this may also impact on the rate of Corporation Tax payable by the company itself.

All of these conflicting factors combine to make the decision whether or not to use a company a highly complex issue. Nevertheless, despite its complexity, it is well worth the effort of undertaking a detailed examination of your own particular circumstances to see whether you have scope to make the substantial tax savings which are available under the right set of conditions.

A detailed examination of the tax benefits and some of the pitfalls of using a company to invest in property is contained in our recently published Taxcafe.co.uk Guide *Using a Property Company to Save Tax*.

In this guide, we show how, using the favourable Corporation Tax regime, a property investor can achieve a significantly higher income than a personal investor. Copies of this guide can be obtained directly from our website.

Appendix A

Tax Rates and Allowances
2002/2003 to 2004/2005

	Rates	Bands, allowances, etc.		
		2002/2003	**2003/2004**	**2004/2005**
		£	£	£
Income tax				
Personal allowance		4,615	4,615	4,745
Starting rate	10%	1,920	1,960	2,020
Basic rate	22%	27,980	28,540	29,380
Higher rate on over	40%	29,900	30,500	31,400
Children's Tax Credit	10%	5,290	Revised*	Revised*
Baby Tax Credit	10%	10,490	Revised*	Revised*
Pension scheme earnings cap		97,200	99,000	102,000
Capital Gains Tax				
Annual exemption:				
Individuals		7,700	7,900	8,200
Trusts		3,850	3,950	4,100
Inheritance Tax				
Nil Rate Band Threshold		250,000	255,000	263,000
Pensioners, etc.				
Age allowance: 65 –74		6,100	6,610	6,830
Age allowance: 75 & over		6,370	6,720	6,950
MCA: born before 6/4/35		5,465	5,565	5,725
MCA: 75 & over		5,535	5,635	5,795
MCA minimum		2,110	2,150	2,210
Income limit		17,900	18,300	18,900
Blind Person's Allowance		1,480	1,510	1,560

* - Replaced by Working Tax Credit and Child Tax Credit, with effect from 6th April 2003.

132

Appendix B
Indexation Relief Rates
(see section 4.9 for application)

Percentages applying to disposals made by individuals after 5th April 1998 of assets acquired (or enhancement expenditure incurred) during:

Month of expenditure	Index'n Rate	Month of expenditure	Index'n Rate
March 1982 or earlier	104.7%	July-85	70.7%
April-82	100.6%	August-85	70.3%
May-82	99.2%	September-85	70.4%
June-82	98.7%	October-85	70.1%
July-82	98.6%	November-85	69.5%
August-82	98.5%	December-85	69.3%
September-82	98.7%	January-86	68.9%
October-82	97.7%	February-86	68.3%
November-82	96.7%	March-86	68.1%
December-82	97.1%	April-86	66.5%
January-83	96.8%	May-86	66.2%
February-83	96.0%	June-86	66.3%
March-83	95.6%	July-86	66.7%
April-83	92.9%	August-86	67.1%
May-83	92.1%	September-86	65.4%
June-83	91.7%	October-86	65.2%
July-83	90.6%	November-86	63.8%
August-83	89.8%	December-86	63.2%
September-83	88.9%	January-87	62.6%
October-83	88.3%	February-87	62.0%
November-83	87.6%	March-87	61.6%
December-83	87.1%	April-87	59.7%
January-84	87.2%	May-87	59.6%
February-84	86.5%	June-87	59.6%
March-84	85.9%	July-87	59.7%
April-84	83.4%	August-87	59.3%
May-84	82.8%	September-87	58.8%
June-84	82.3%	October-87	58.0%
July-84	82.5%	November-87	57.3%
August-84	80.8%	December-87	57.4%
September-84	80.4%	January-88	57.4%
October-84	79.3%	February-88	56.8%
November-84	78.8%	March-88	56.2%
December-84	78.9%	April-88	54.5%
January-85	78.3%	May-88	53.1%
February-85	76.9%	June-88	52.5%
March-85	75.2%	July-88	52.4%
April-85	71.6%	August-88	50.7%
May-85	70.8%	September-88	50.0%
June-85	70.4%	October-88	48.5%

Appendix B (cont'd)

Month of expenditure	Index'n Rate	Month of expenditure	Index'n Rate
November-88	47.8%	September-92	16.6%
December-88	47.4%	October-92	16.2%
January-89	46.5%	November-92	16.4%
February-89	45.4%	December-92	16.8%
March-89	44.8%	January-93	17.9%
April-89	42.3%	February-93	17.1%
May-89	41.4%	March-93	16.7%
June-89	40.9%	April-93	15.6%
July-89	40.8%	May-93	15.2%
August-89	40.4%	June-93	15.3%
September-89	39.5%	July-93	15.6%
October-89	38.4%	August-93	15.1%
November-89	37.2%	September-93	14.6%
December-89	36.9%	October-93	14.7%
January-90	36.1%	November-93	14.8%
February-90	35.3%	December-93	14.6%
March-90	33.9%	January-94	15.1%
April-90	30.0%	February-94	14.4%
May-90	28.8%	March-94	14.1%
June-90	28.3%	April-94	12.8%
July-90	28.2%	May-94	12.4%
August-90	26.9%	June-94	12.4%
September-90	25.8%	July-94	12.9%
October-90	24.8%	August-94	12.4%
November-90	25.1%	September-94	12.1%
December-90	25.2%	October-94	12.0%
January-91	24.9%	November-94	11.9%
February-91	24.2%	December-94	11.4%
March-91	23.7%	January-95	11.4%
April-91	22.2%	February-95	10.7%
May-91	21.8%	March-95	10.2%
June-91	21.3%	April-95	9.1%
July-91	21.5%	May-95	8.7%
August-91	21.3%	June-95	8.5%
September-91	20.8%	July-95	9.1%
October-91	20.4%	August-95	8.5%
November-91	19.9%	September-95	8.0%
December-91	19.8%	October-95	8.5%
January-92	19.9%	November-95	8.5%
February-92	19.3%	December-95	7.9%
March-92	18.9%	January-96	8.3%
April-92	17.1%	February-96	7.8%
May-92	16.7%	March-96	7.3%
June-92	16.7%	April-96	6.6%
July-92	17.1%	May-96	6.3%
August-92	17.1%	June-96	6.3%

Appendix B (cont'd)

Month of expenditure Index'n Rate

Month of expenditure	Index'n Rate
July-96	6.7%
August-96	6.2%
September-96	5.7%
October-96	5.7%
November-96	5.7%
December-96	5.3%
January-97	5.3%
February-97	4.9%
March-97	4.6%
April-97	4.0%
May-97	3.6%
June-97	3.2%
July-97	3.2%
August-97	2.6%
September-97	2.1%
October-97	1.9%
November-97	1.9%
December-97	1.6%
January-98	1.9%
February-98	1.4%
March-98	1.1%
April 1998 or later	0.0%

Need Affordable & Expert Tax Planning Advice?

Try Our Unique Question & Answer Service

The purpose of this guide is to provide you with detailed guidance on how to pay less Income Tax and Capital Gains Tax on your property business.

Ultimately you may want to take further action or obtain advice personal to your circumstances.

Taxcafe.co.uk has a unique online tax advice service that provides access to highly qualified tax professionals at an affordable rate.

No matter how complex your question, we will provide you with detailed tax planning guidance through this service. The cost is just £69.95.

To find out more go to **www.taxcafe.co.uk** and click the Tax Questions button.

Pay Less Tax!

... with help from Taxcafe's unique tax guides, software and Q&A service

All products available online at www.taxcafe.co.uk

- ➢ **How to Avoid Property Tax.** Essential reading for property investors who want to know all the tips and tricks to follow to pay less tax on their property profits.

- ➢ **Using a Property Company to Save Tax.** How to massively increase your profits by using a property company... plus all the traps to avoid.

- ➢ **How to Avoid Inheritance Tax.** A-Z of Inheritance Tax planning, with clear explanations & numerous examples. Covers simple & sophisticated tax planning.

- ➢ **Non Resident & Offshore Tax Planning.** How to exploit non-resident tax status to reduce your tax bill, plus advice on using offshore trusts and companies.

- ➢ **Incorporate & Save Tax.** Everything you need to know about the tax benefits of using a company to run your business.

- ➢ **Bonus vs Dividends.** Shows how shareholder/directors of companies can save thousands in tax by choosing the optimal mix of bonus and dividends.

- ➢ **Selling a Business.** A potential minefield with numerous traps to avoid but significant tax saving opportunities.

➢ **How to Claim Tax Credits.** Even families with higher incomes can make successful tax credit claims. This guide shows how much you can claim and how to go about it.

➢ **Property Capital Gains Tax Calculator.** Unique software that performs complex Capital Gains Tax calculations in seconds.

➢ **Fast Tax Advice**. We offer a unique Tax Question Service. Answers from highly qualified specialist tax advisers. Just click the Tax Questions button on our site.

Essential Property Investment Guides

...written by leading experts and packed with tips & tricks of the trade

All products available online at www.taxcafe.co.uk

- ➤ **An Insider's Guide to Successful Property Investing.** Little-known secrets of successful property investors. A "must read" for anyone interested in making big profits and avoiding costly mistakes.

- ➤ **An Insider's Guide to Successful Property Investing - Part II.** How the experts make millions by using simple but clever techniques to find, buy, manage and sell property.

- ➤ **No Money Down Property Millions.** Written by a wealthy property investor, this entertaining and brilliantly clever guide shows you how to invest in property without using any of your own money.

- ➤ **The Successful Landlord's Handbook.** Definitive guide for Buy to Let investors. Covers: sourcing cheap property, using borrowed money to earn big capital gains, finding quality tenants, earning high rents, legal traps, letting agents, and lots more...

- ➤ **63 Common Defects in Investment Property & How to Spot Them.** With full colour illustrations, this unique guide will save you thousands by steering you clear of no-hope property investments and towards bargain-priced gems.

- ➤ **Property Auctions Bargains.** One of the best-kept secrets of successful property investors is to buy at rock-bottom prices at auction. This A-Z guide tells you everything you need to know.

www.taxcafe.co.uk

DISCLAIMER BY TAXCAFE UK LIMITED

Printed in the United Kingdom
by Lightning Source UK Ltd.
102956UKS00001B/298-372

9 781904 608134